At Issue

Manufacturing Jobs in the US

Other Books in the At Issue Series:

At Issue

Manufacturing Jobs in the US

Amy Francis, Book Editor

GREENHAVEN PRESS
A part of Gale, Cengage Learning

GALE
CENGAGE Learning·

Farmington Hills, Mich • San Francisco • New York • Waterville, Maine
Meriden, Conn • Mason, Ohio • Chicago

Patricia Coryell, *Vice President & Publisher, New Products & GVRL*
Douglas Dentino, *Manager, New Products*
Judy Galens, *Acquisitions Editor*

For more information, contact:
Greenhaven Press
27500 Drake Rd.
Farmington Hills, MI 48331-3535
Or you can visit our Internet site at gale.cengage.com

For product information and technology assistance, contact us at

Gale Customer Support, 1-800-877-4253
For permission to use material from this text or product, submit all requests online at www.cengage.com/permissions

Further permissions questions can be emailed to permissionrequest@cengage.com

Articles in Greenhaven Press anthologies are often edited for length to meet page requirements. In addition, original titles of these works are changed to clearly present the main thesis and to explicitly indicate the author's opinion. Every effort is made to ensure that Greenhaven Press accurately reflects the original intent of the authors. Every effort has been made to trace the owners of copyrighted material.

Cover image © Images.com/Corbis.

LIBRARY OF CONGRESS CATALOGING-IN-PUBLICATION DATA

Manufacturing jobs in the US / Amy Francis, book editor.
    pages cm. -- (At issue)
    Includes bibliographical references and index.
    ISBN 978-0-7377-7173-2 (hardcover) -- ISBN 978-0-7377-7174-9 (pbk.)
    1. Manufacturing industries--United States. 2. Labor market--United States. 3. Labor supply--United States. I. Francis, Amy.
    HD9725.M358 2015
    331.7'670973--dc23
                                                                    2014041176

Printed in Mexico
1 2 3 4 5 6 7 19 18 17 16 15

Contents

Introduction

Americans who seek out items manufactured in the United States give many reasons for doing so, including supporting local economic development, perceived higher quality of US manufactured goods, and higher US safety standards and oversight. Additionally, many point to deplorable working conditions in overseas manufacturing facilities, often referred to as sweatshops. Some of the problems workers face in these facilities are unfair wages, long hours, difficult and dangerous working conditions, the illegal use of child labor, and the inability to organize unions. Following a series of tragedies at manufacturing plants in South Asia, a popular location for the manufacture of US-destined goods, the plight of these sweatshop workers received major media attention.

The largest incident to date occurred April 24, 2013, when the Rana Plaza factory in Bangladesh collapsed killing more than 1,100 workers and injuring approximately 2,500, but this was only one incident in a series that included a number of disasters, mostly fires. In total, an estimated 1,800 workers were killed in factories in Bangladesh alone since 2005. Many thousands more were injured and an estimated four million are still currently employed in textile manufacturing in Bangladesh.

Raveena Aulakh, a Canadian journalist, went to Bangladesh to experience factory work first hand. As she wrote in the *Toronto Star*, Aulakh was trained by a nine-year-old factory worker, Meem, for her job snipping away loose threads from men's shirts. Aulakh writes, "It was back-breaking, it was finger numbing. It was particularly rage-inducing. . . . Not because it was painfully hard work but because children like Meem hunched over hour after hour, squinted at the threads, cleaned one collar after another, one cuff after another, one arm piece after another until the piles were depleted."[1] These girls, she reported, worked twelve hours a day and earned only $25 a month.

As images from the tragedies and stories like Aulakh's circulated, many Americans called on retailers to pull out of the countries where they were manufacturing their goods, while others began boycott campaigns. Tufts University economics professor Drusilla Brown argues, however, that boycotting these retailers or retailers pulling their business out of Bangladesh isn't going to help. In an interview for Minnesota Public Radio, Brown states that American companies should "stay in there and work it through so that all the benefits of economic growth that come with sourcing from developing countries become available to these poor locations. . . . As attractive as low wages and long hours might seem to a firm trying to cut costs, we've found a lot of evidence that better working conditions actually correlate with higher productivity and higher profits. It definitely doesn't have to be about exploitation."[2]

Likewise, Racheal Meiers, director of HERproject, which brings health and financial education to women working in factories in Asia and Africa, writes in an *HBR Blog Network* post, "Despite the risks, women actually want to *work*. . . . Factory jobs give millions of women what they can't get anywhere else: a salaried wage. With it, they can begin to exert control over their future. Factory work isn't just about making clothes; it's also about a potential path toward gender equality."[3]

1. Raveena Aulakh, "I Got Hired at a Bangladesh Sweatshop," *Toronto Star*, October 11, 2013. www.thestar.com/news/world/clothesonyourback/2013/10/11/i_got_hired_at_a _bangladesh_sweatshop_meet_my_9yearold_boss.html.
2. Quoted in Martin Moylan, "Retailers, Including Target, Grapple with Unsafe Foreign Factories," Minnesota Public Radio, August 5, 2013. www.mprnews.org/story/2013/08 /05/business/target-developing-nation-unsafe-factories.
3. Racheal Meiers, "The Other Women's Movement: Factory Workers in the Developing World," *HBR Blog Network*, May 28, 2013. http://blogs.hbr.org/2013/05/the-other -womens-movement-fact.

This argument doesn't sit well with everyone, however. William Lawrence, dean and professor of American Church History, Perkins School of Theology, Southern Methodist University, stated in the *Dallas Morning News*, "Only those who have never labored in such conditions would allow themselves to view sweatshops of the world as a door to opportunity for entering the global economy. Only those who never imagine their children finding careers in such settings could treat the human beings who labor there as commodities to be used maximally and compensated minimally until they are replaced by the next laborer willing to put life and limb at risk."[4]

Some retailers did respond by signing the 2013 Accord on Fire and Building Safety in Bangladesh, a legally binding agreement between international trade unions and retailers to implement a program for health and safety measures in Bangladesh. The program is reported to be having an impact. During a June 2014 debate held at the University of Manchester, most Bangladeshi panelists agreed the accord was leading to positive changes. Jenny Holdcroft, policy director at Industri-All Global Union, stated that the accord "has seized the opportunity and shown that it is possible to find another way of doing things . . . you can have industry-wide reform and that everyone can work together."[5] It will be years, however, before the results of the 2013 accord experiment could be fully realized, and Bangladesh is only one of the countries making goods for sale in American markets. Whether or not people should buy from retailers who source their products from international manufacturing factories will likely continue to be debated.

4. Quoted in Bill McKenzie, "Texas Faith: Should Americans Boycott Sweatshops in Places like Bangladesh?," *Dallas Morning News*, May 23, 2013. http://religionblog .dallasnews.com/2013/05/texas-faith-should-americans-boycott-sweatshops-in-places -like-bangladesh.html.

5. Quoted in "Buying with a Conscience: Should We Buy Clothes from Bangladesh?," Development@Manchester, June 16, 2014. http://developmentatmanchester.com/tag /justice.

Meanwhile, for some Americans, the depth of these problems is yet another reason to buy US-manufactured goods. US manufacturing, however, is not without its own problems and controversies, many of which are debated in the following pages of *At Issue: Manufacturing Jobs in the US.*

1

Manufacturing Is Growing Across the United States

Mark Crawford

Mark Crawford is the author of five nonfiction books and numerous articles. He is based in Madison, Wisconsin.

Many states are growing their manufacturing sectors, bringing valuable jobs back to America and helping regions severely impacted by the recession to make a comeback. The most successful states have a combination of workforce training programs, a diverse manufacturing base, flexible incentive packages for businesses, and supportive local governments. These businesses in turn are making advancements in research and technology. As a result, American manufacturing is once again able to compete globally, and the industry will help aid the financial recovery of the nation.

Manufacturing is the backbone of America. It's in our blood. Americans know how to build—it's how we forged a nation, won two world wars, put men on the moon, and shaped the "new economy." American workers are among the most productive in the world. With new advances in technology, lean manufacturing techniques, and best practices, American manufacturing is becoming cost-competitive with offshore locations, resulting in more companies bringing their operations back to the United States (or near-shoring to Mexico).

Continued Improvement

According to the Institute of Supply Management (ISM), American manufacturing continues to improve. The ISM recently reported that manufacturing activity expanded in January 2013 for the second consecutive month and that the overall national economy grew for the 44th consecutive month. The Purchasing Managers Index (PMI) registered 53.1 percent, an increase of 2.9 percent from December's [2012] value of 50.2 percent. All five PMI component indices registered above 50 percent in January—including employment, one of the most critical indicators.

The PMI employment index jumped from 51.9 percent to 54.0 percent in January 2013. This is especially significant because manufacturing companies learned how to be incredibly efficient during the Great Recession, doing more with far less—this means manufacturers are reaching their limits and must hire more to keep up with new orders.

So, which are the top manufacturing states that are leading us out of recession? We compiled this list from the Bureau of Labor Statistics' (BLS) November 2012 rankings for the top 10 states in total manufacturing jobs and the top 10 for manufacturing's share of non-farm employment, as well as the National Association of Manufacturers' [NAM] top 10 states for manufacturing's share of GSP [Gross State Product] (2011).

Arkansas' workers continue to impress employers with their work ethic, skills, productivity, and low turnover rates.

This simple approach identified 19 states that are leading the U.S. in manufacturing prosperity: Alabama, Arkansas, California, Illinois, Indiana, Iowa, Kansas, Kentucky, Louisiana, Michigan, Mississippi, New York, North Carolina, Ohio, Oregon, Pennsylvania, South Carolina, Texas, and Wisconsin.

Shared traits include a diversified manufacturing base, positive business climate, flexible incentive packages, outstanding work force development programs, and highly proactive local and state governments that support manufacturing. Below are manufacturing snapshots of each state that show how they are strengthening their industries and contributing to our national economic recovery.

Alabama. Key manufacturing sectors in Alabama are aerospace/defense, automotive, agricultural products/food distribution, metals, forestry products, chemicals, biosciences, and information technology. Much of the state's manufacturing output is exported—in fact, 2012 was a record-breaking year with $19.5 billion in exported goods, an increase of almost 10 percent over 2011. "This shows that Alabama's economy continues to improve and we are making gains in exporting to countries all over the world," says Governor Robert Bentley. "The products made in Alabama are second to none, and we have a world-class work force." . . .

Arkansas. Arkansas continues to diversify its manufacturing base by adding advanced manufacturing jobs. Top sectors are food and beverage, paper, transportation, machinery, wood products, chemicals, plastics and rubber, and apparel.

Arkansas' highly skilled work force and favorable business climate, combined with its research and education opportunities, make the state an attractive location for manufacturing. Arkansas' workers continue to impress employers with their work ethic, skills, productivity, and low turnover rates. Arkansas' labor force is projected to grow by 4 percent by 2015. . . .

California. California is a national leader in job creation, with over 257,000 private-sector jobs created in 2012. Its private-sector growth rate of 2.2 percent is outpacing the national average, and its unemployment rate of 9.8 percent is the lowest it has been in almost four years—due in part to the resurgence of manufacturing in the state. More than 1.2 million people are employed in manufacturing jobs, the most in the nation, according to the Bureau of Labor Statistics.

The National Association of Manufacturers (NAM) notes that manufacturers in California account for 11.2 percent of the total GSP (2011), employing almost 9 percent of the work force. Total overall output from manufacturing was $229.9 billion in 2011, significantly higher than in any other state. Nearly $138 billion of that output was exported—an important figure because more than 22 percent of California's manufacturing employment depends on exports. . . .

[Indiana's] central location and excellent transportation network—combined with a skilled and dedicated work force—make it an ideal location for manufacturing.

Illinois. Illinois is a major producer of chemicals, machinery, computers and electronics, rubber and plastic products, and fabricated metals. Manufacturing totaled more than $86.5 billion in output in 2011 and employed nearly 600,000 workers as of November 2012.

"We have experienced significant growth in manufacturing in recent years, which has created tremendous opportunities for growing our economy and creating more jobs," says Adam Pollet, acting director for the Illinois Department of Commerce and Economic Opportunity.

Top manufacturers in the state include Caterpillar, Deere & Company, Motorola, Navistar, Chrysler/Fiat, Ford, and Mitsubishi. Newer advanced manufacturing sectors such as aerospace and pharmaceuticals are also becoming established. . . .

Indiana. Indiana combines traditional production with progressive technology to create an attractive environment for manufacturers. The state's central location and excellent transportation network—combined with a skilled and dedicated work force—make it an ideal location for manufacturing. Top manufacturing sectors include automotive, parts and transportation equipment, metals, machinery, plastics and rubber, chemicals, and computers and electronics.

Nearly 17 percent of the Indiana non-farm work force is employed in manufacturing (the most of any state according to BLS statistics for November 2012). Manufacturing employment grew 4.2 percent from October 2011 to October 2012, more than double the national average of 1.6 percent. Since 2010, Indiana has added the third-most manufacturing jobs of any state in the country—an impressive 9 percent growth rate....

Iowa. Iowa's $27.6 billion advanced manufacturing industry is the state's largest single business sector—with more than 6,000 manufacturers operating 6,400 factories, employing 200,000 workers, and generating more than 18 percent of Iowa's total gross state product (GSP) in 2011, according to NAM. During the past decade Iowa's manufacturing GSP has grown at an impressive inflation-adjusted rate of 9.2 percent.

Advanced manufacturing is a major factor in the Kansas economy—especially aviation and aerospace.

Leading industries include industrial metal processing, automation precision machinery, environment control systems, digital and electronic devices, and power generation equipment. Other top sectors are aerospace and defense, industrial chemicals, construction components, commercial and industrial motor vehicles, food ingredients, printing and packaging, pharmaceuticals, and medical devices and products....

Kansas. Total Kansas GSP in 2011 was $130.9 billion. Manufacturing accounted for more than $18.4 billion of that, or about 14 percent. As of November 2012, 167,000 workers were employed in manufacturing in the state—more than 12 percent of the state's non-farm work force.

Advanced manufacturing is a major factor in the Kansas economy—especially aviation and aerospace. For example, Wichita manufacturers produce more than 40 percent of the world's general aviation aircraft. Major aircraft companies with Kansas operations include Hawker Beechcraft, Cessna, Spirit Aerosystems, and Bombardier Learjet. Nearly 60 percent of the state's manufacturing work force is employed in this vital sector. General Motors, which manufactures Chevrolet and Buick in the Kansas City area, is another key employer.

Bioscience is a rapidly growing field in Kansas, including an "animal health corridor" that runs through central Kansas. Here major companies and research centers conduct cutting-edge research and innovation on new products for animal health and nutrition. This corridor accounts for almost one third of total world sales in the $19 billion global animal health market. Currently more than 16,000 employees work in the biosciences. The Kansas Bioscience Authority is investing $580 million to further support R&D [research and development] and commercialization opportunities in this field and accelerate cluster growth. . . .

Kentucky. Manufacturing is Kentucky's third-largest employment sector—nearly one out of every eight non-agricultural jobs in Kentucky is in manufacturing. In 2012, 232 manufacturing facilities announced new locations or expansions in the state, which will contribute over $2.25 billion in capital investment and create about 6,700 new jobs. One quarter of these new projects are related to the automotive industry, creating nearly one third of all new manufacturing jobs in the state. According to the U.S. Bureau of Labor Statistics, Kentucky gained 1,400 manufacturing jobs from December 2011 to December 2012—among the most in the nation. . . .

"Manufacturing is a crucial sector of our economy, representing about 16.5 percent of Kentucky's GSP," says Erik Dunnigan, commissioner for Kentucky's Department for Business Development. "The diversity of our manufacturing base is also vital to our growth. More than 2,400 manufacturing facilities across Kentucky produce everything from automobiles and aerospace parts to food, beverage, and paper products and everything in between," Dunnigan continues. "The Commonwealth's reputation for meeting and exceeding industry needs, and providing companies with a skilled and available work force to meet the demands of a global economy, continues to fuel our manufacturing success."

Louisiana. Manufacturing accounts for about 25 percent of Louisiana's GSP, according to NAM. The state has a history of both traditional and advanced manufacturing, especially related to natural resources and energy. Affordable energy is a big reason companies choose Louisiana. Louisiana's highly developed pipeline infrastructure, combined with an abundant supply of historically low-priced natural gas, makes the state an attractive location for industrial projects. . . .

"Louisiana's reputation as a low-cost business environment and a critically important energy state opens doors for us," says Louisiana Economic Development Secretary Stephen Moret. "But what seals many manufacturing deals is our work force development program—LED FastStart—and our targeted incentives that reward job creation, facility modernization, and capital expansions."

Michigan. "Michigan is a leader in making things and making things work," says Governor Rick Snyder. "Very few locations in the world can match our world-leading bases in manufacturing, R&D, engineering, and high-skilled talent. These advantages—combined with the bold reforms we have made to our business climate—are generating new opportunities for manufacturers of all sizes and in all industries."

For example, business taxes are lower than at any time in decades. The state's flat 6 percent tax for "C" corporations is among the lowest in the nation and has slashed business costs by 83 percent. According to the Tax Foundation, a nonpartisan tax research group, Michigan's overall corporate tax ranking is now 12th best in the country. The Michigan Economic Development Corporation also spends $150 million annually in incentives and assistance, along with another $100 million for loan support to small and mid-size businesses.

Sustainable energy—especially biomass—is an emerging industry for Mississippi.

Durable goods manufacturing output in Michigan increased 41 percent in the past two years, reaching a value of $55.9 billion in 2012. Although a variety of manufacturing industries has contributed to this resurgence, automotive is still king. Michigan is home to more than 370 vehicle-related R&D and technical centers, including research, product development, or production facilities for eight of the 10 largest OEMs [original equipment manufacturers], as well as a vast network of automotive suppliers. . . .

Mississippi. Mississippi continues to show a positive economic trend, with a 2 percent gain projected for 2013. Manufacturing companies, especially automakers, are key drivers for this economic momentum and employ 12.5 percent of the state's total non-farm work force, according to the BLS (November 2012). . . .

Sustainable energy—especially biomass—is an emerging industry for Mississippi with high growth potential. The state is rich in biomass resources, largely derived from the wood products and paper industries. Biomass is processed to create a feedstock that can be burned efficiently to generate steam and electricity. Leading private-sector firms continue to invest in biomass research and development in the state. Most recently, British-based Drax Biomass International announced it would construct an $80 million wood pellet production facility in Gloster to provide fuel for its power plant in England.

"With our abundance of biomass resources, Mississippi offers important advantages to businesses that rely on biomass for their operations," says Brent Christensen, executive director of the Mississippi Development Authority. "Drax Biomass' decision to locate its plant in Gloster is exciting news for all of Southwest Mississippi."

New York. Manufacturing remains a key element of the economy in every part of New York—food/beverages, petroleum and coal products, textiles, machinery, and primary metal manufacturing are especially showing strong gains. New York's strengths—its proximity to markets, skilled work force, and higher education and R&D institutions—continue to make the state an attractive place to do business and capitalize on new advanced manufacturing opportunities.

"Governor [Andrew] Cuomo is committed to growing New York's manufacturing industry and creating jobs," indicates Empire State Development (ESD) President and CEO Kenneth Adams. "From investing in traditional manufacturing sectors to advanced manufacturing industries, ESD is focused on making New York State the place to be for manufacturing." . . .

North Carolina. North Carolina has a long history of manufacturing excellence—from its traditional, natural-resources-based industries to the innovative, high-tech R&D and commercialization that give its research centers, such as Research Triangle Park, a world-class reputation.

Manufacturing is the largest driver of North Carolina's economic growth (35 percent) coming out of the recession. Almost 20 percent of the GSP is attributed to manufacturing by NAM (2011). Nearly 440,000 employees work in manufacturing, which represents 11 percent of the state's non-farm work force, according to the BLS (November 2012). Over the last two years North Carolina has added 7,200 net manufacturing jobs.

"Some companies are coming to North Carolina because of reshoring initiatives," says North Carolina Deputy Secretary of Commerce Dale Carroll. "They realize that North Carolina's geographic proximity to customers and supply chains, highly skilled and productive work force, and reasonable transportation, labor, and logistics costs make it possible to be cost-competitive with overseas locations like China.". . .

Ohio. According to the U.S. Bureau of Labor Statistics, Ohio gained 50,000 manufacturing jobs from 2009 through December 2012. Overall, manufacturing has accounted for about a quarter of the state's job growth over the past two years, while increasing its output by about 12 percent ($8 billion). Over the last 12 months, the hottest manufacturing sectors for jobs were transportation equipment (1,700), food manufacturing (1,900), and plastics and polymers (1,200). Other key industries on the rebound are chemicals, structural steel, and fabricated metals.

"We are seeing the resurgence of Ohio's manufacturing industry, which is creating economic prosperity and jobs for Ohioans," says Christiane Schmenk, director of the Ohio Development Services Agency. "From automotive to advanced manufacturing technologies such as fuel cells, we are implementing more resources to support Ohio manufacturers."

Global companies like Boeing and Intel are undergoing billion-dollar expansions [in Oregon].

These resources include expanded services from the Manufacturing Extension Partnership program, which now provides a broader regional model with five regional centers and has increased outreach to smaller manufacturers with 50 or fewer workers. The state also introduced the Energy Efficiency Program for Manufacturers, which has invested more than $24 million in Ohio's manufacturing sector to help hundreds of companies reduce their energy consumption, improving cost efficiencies and making them more competitive in the global marketplace. . . .

Oregon. Manufacturing represented 28.7 percent of Oregon's GSP in 2011 (NAM)—the largest share in the nation. And, the American Institute for Economic Research recently recognized Oregon as the best state in the nation for manufacturing. With a focus on quality and adding value in advanced manufacturing products, Oregon has developed and maintained a skilled work force ready for the modern manufacturing environment.

"With the number of Oregonians employed in manufacturing at 10 percent and growing, making high-quality products for the entire world is one of our state's greatest economic strengths," says Tim McCabe, director of Business Oregon.

Top manufacturing sectors are computers and electronics, food, wood products, fabricated metal, transportation equipment, and machinery. Global companies like Boeing and Intel are undergoing billion-dollar expansions. . . .

Pennsylvania. Pennsylvania's manufacturing companies are leading the state's economic resurgence following the Great Recession. With gross state product (GSP) exceeding $70 billion, Pennsylvania manufacturers account for more than 12 percent of the state's GSP (NAM). Productivity is on the rise as companies continue to adopt process innovations and new technologies, including automation and additive manufacturing.

"Manufacturing in the U.S. is definitely changing," indicates Pennsylvania Governor Tom Corbett. "It is important for governors to continue to learn so they can determine the best way forward, ensuring good businesses and rewarding jobs for their states."

Pennsylvania's economy is highly diversified—no single industry accounts for more than 5 percent of the total number of businesses in the state. Key sectors include transportation, metal machining and fabrication, glass, chemicals, and plastics. These industry sectors are also well positioned to support growth in emerging markets such as energy, medical devices, and life sciences. . . .

South Carolina. Big companies like BMW, Boeing, Continental, and Michelin have invested more than $7 billion in new projects in South Carolina over the last two years, creating about 21,000 jobs since January 2010. This represents a greater than 10 percent employment gain—one of the best in the country. . . .

In January 2013, South Carolina was recognized by IBM-Plant Location International (IBM-PLI) as the top state for jobs linked to foreign investment. South Carolina placed first above Texas and North Carolina, which were ranked second and third, respectively, in the 2012 report.

"Hundreds of foreign firms employ tens of thousands of residents throughout our state, creating wealth and helping make the communities they're in sustainable," says Secretary of Commerce Bobby Hitt. "The IBM-PLI report's ranking is another confirmation that people are taking notice of the economic development successes we've had here in the Palmetto State."

Texas. Texas has a highly diversified economy, ranging from rich energy resources to high-tech industries like semiconductors, electronics, aerospace, and information and communications technology. Oil and gas recovery and production technologies continue to evolve, expanding the extent of productive reservoirs and reducing the price of natural gas—a big advantage for industries that rely heavily on natural gas as an energy source for manufacturing.

According to the Texas Workforce Commission (TWC), Texas manufacturing employed 850,300 in December 2012—about 8 percent of the state's nonagricultural employment. Texas added approximately 5,700 manufacturing jobs in 2012 and has consistently increased the total number of manufacturing jobs every year since 2009. . . .

Wisconsin. Wisconsin's manufacturing companies employ about 17 percent of the state's non-farm work force, according to the BLS (November 2012)—nearly twice the national average (9 percent). The state is home to 11,453 manufacturers that employ more than 450,000 (BLS, Nov. 2012) workers and support thousands more jobs in other industries.

Key "driver industries" include wood products, transportation equipment, and electrical equipment. Wisconsin's top three categories for international exports are industrial machinery equipment, electrical machinery, and medical/scientific instruments.

"We're seeing significantly improved health of our manufacturing sector compared to two years ago," comments Lee Swindall, vice president of Business and Industry Development for the Wisconsin Economic Development Corporation. "Wisconsin manufacturers are investing in new capital equipment as they experience rising demand for their products overseas." . . .

"Wisconsin's strong and diverse manufacturing sector has helped our state tremendously during the economic downturn and put us in a strong position going forward," adds Swindall. "We need more skilled workers in Wisconsin for the manufacturing sector. We're addressing that challenge through a number of initiatives, including partnering with our technical college system and reaching out to high school students about the benefits of a career in manufacturing."

2

US Manufacturing Only Has Jobs for the Skilled Few

A. Gary Shilling

A. Gary Shilling is an American financial analyst, columnist for Bloomberg View, and frequent contributor to The New York Times, Forbes, *and* Wall Street Journal. *He is also the author of* The Age of Deleveraging: Investment Strategies for a Decade of Slow Growth and Deflation.

The United States is not able to compete with lower labor costs overseas. The rise in US manufacturing is due to the increased use of technology, which requires only a few highly trained workers. Furthermore, there is a shortage of engineers and other highly skilled workers, which will require that the country issue more work visas to foreign professionals. Despite recent optimism, the reality is that few American jobs will be created even as the manufacturing sector recovers in the years ahead.

Even with the recent strength in the U.S. manufacturing sector, labor-intensive industries won't return to the U.S. as long as the huge labor compensation gaps persist with Asian and other developing countries. Sure, there will be niches created when quick delivery, changes in fashion and other developments require production to be close by.

The majority of what could be rapid growth in U.S. manufacturing will probably come from capital-intensive, robotics-intensive production that doesn't require many people. Those employed in this area will need considerable skills. Furthermore, these are the industries that show rapid productivity growth as new technologies are introduced. But when productivity growth is robust, output will rise substantially without much increase in employment.

There are concerns about the lack of engineers and other professionals who make sophisticated manufacturing possible, especially as highly skilled members of the postwar generation reach retirement age. In 2008, the latest available data, 4 percent of bachelor's degrees in the U.S. were in engineering, compared with 17 percent in all of Asia and 34 percent in China. That means that more H-1B visas allowing foreign professionals to work in the U.S. will be awarded. A Senate-passed immigration measure increases the number of these visas to 110,000 a year, from 65,000 now.

Industrial robots can operate 24 hours a day with no coffee breaks. Their cost compared with human labor has fallen 50 percent since 1990.

3-D Printing

One of the most exciting new technologies is additive manufacturing, popularly known as 3-D printing, which uses layers of materials ranging from wood pulp to cobalt to human tissue to make three-dimensional objects of almost any shape from a digital model. Machines have been developed that can print more than 1,000 materials, and the layers can be mixed to embed sensors and circuitry such as those used for hearing aids and motion-sensing gloves.

Another form of additive manufacturing is cold spraying, in which metallic particles are blasted at high speeds and fuse into the desired shapes.

Industrial robots can operate 24 hours a day with no coffee breaks. Their cost compared with human labor has fallen

50 percent since 1990. Thanks to high-technology manufacturing, Boston Consulting Group estimated that 30 percent of Chinese exports to the U.S. could be economically produced domestically by 2020.

The U.S. won't enjoy much of an advantage from lower energy costs. Crude oil prices are reasonably uniform throughout the world. The U.S. benchmark is West Texas Intermediate [WTI]; Brent is the standard elsewhere, but the two move pretty much together. There have been differences, specifically the recent discount of WTI because leaping U.S. output was bottled up at Cushing, Oklahoma, until pipelines could be reversed to let it flow to the Gulf of Mexico. Then the gap closed.

Because of the high cost of liquefying and shipping natural gas, however, its markets are localized. U.S. gas is about $3.60 per million British thermal units, from $13.58 in 2008. The commodity fetches about $10 in Europe and $15 to $20 in Asia. This helps U.S. industries such as nitrogen fertilizer manufacturing and petrochemicals that are heavy users of natural gas. Still, the advantage isn't as great as many believe.

The days of new auto plants that employ 5,000 semiskilled workers are unlikely to return.

For all manufacturing sectors, energy inputs, only one of which is natural gas, accounted for only 1.9 percent of the value of output, as of 2011, the latest data available. The largest manufacturing users are nonmetallic mineral products (6.8 percent), primary metals (6.2 percent) and paper (6.6 percent). Surprisingly, energy only accounts for 5.6 percent of utility output. It is more important in some other nonmanufacturing industries such as farms (8.8 percent) and transportation by air (25.8 percent), rail (12.6 percent), water (31.8 percent) and truck (18.2 percent).

Energy Costs

Many factors besides energy costs affect industrial production, but within manufacturing, energy-intensive industries have underperformed in terms of industrial output in recent years.

Energy usage is equivalent only to about 17 percent of U.S. gross domestic product as the economy becomes more service-oriented and energy conservation increases. By contrast, in China, energy usage equals about 27 percent of GDP.

If U.S. manufacturing is enjoying a renaissance, it is one that's focused on technology and capital-intensive production. The days of new auto plants that employ 5,000 semi-skilled workers are unlikely to return. Indeed, the recent increase in manufacturing employment has been driven by economic recovery, and there's no evidence of a big job pickup thanks to advanced manufacturing, cheap energy or the return of jobs from abroad.

3

US Manufacturing Forecasts Are Overly Optimistic

Manning & Napier

Manning & Napier is a US investment company based in Rochester, New York.

Growth in the US manufacturing sector has not been as rapid as anticipated. Many optimistic reports argued that problems in overseas manufacturing—including uncertain labor costs, lack of intellectual property protection, quality control issues, and additional transportation expenses—would lead to a return of manufacturing jobs in America. However, there are still many risks for manufacturing in the United States, including an aging workforce and policy changes with regard to tax rates and trade restrictions. While continued growth in US manufacturing is expected, it is likely that the growth will be slow.

Over two years have passed since we introduced the U.S. Manufacturing Renaissance theme in our Outlook Series [in 2012]. At that time, we detailed initial signs of a pick-up in domestic manufacturing, driven by both a return of formerly outsourced production as well as an expansion in goods for export. This trend was being driven by a narrowing of U.S. labor cost differentials versus other nations, combined with several other competitive advantages (e.g., favorable energy prices, largest domestic market in the world, a culture of innovation, excellent universities, a well-trained workforce, strict intellectual property rights, and good infrastructure). We also noted the existence of meaningful headwinds to a resurgence of U.S. manufacturing, including a shortage of high-skilled workers, and policy risks. Our conclusion back in 2012 was that this phenomenon had the potential to be a positive contributor to economic growth in the U.S., but that it had not yet evolved far enough to alter our expectation for an ongoing period of slow growth.

The Manufacturing Renaissance theme and overall economic growth have largely tracked the expectations we established two years ago. However, there have been some welcome surprises to the upside in certain elements to this theme, including the energy sector. This month [June 2014], we revisit our original work on this topic to provide an update on the progress of U.S. manufacturing and the implications for growth from here. In preview, slow growth remains our base case, although we continue to believe the Manufacturing Renaissance is a viable trend which still has the potential to evolve into a long-term engine of economic growth.

Checking Up on the Manufacturing Renaissance

Manufacturing activity as a share of U.S. GDP [gross domestic product] has been in steady decline for several decades. While manufacturing's output and value-add has continued trending upward, its trajectory has been more gradual than other sectors, resulting in its falling share of output. Over the past two years, there have been signs that this downward trend is abating. In fact, this expansion was the first noteworthy increase in manufacturing's value-add share of U.S. GDP since the 1980's (the blip in 1997–1998 is due to a change in methodology). Durables have recovered much more robustly than non-durables, especially in Computer and Electronics, Motor Vehicles, and Machinery, passing their pre-recession peak in the third quarter of 2011. [1]

There are numerous recent examples of companies returning manufacturing activities to (or increasing manufacturing
in) the U.S. The nation's share of global manufacturing output has stabilized at around 20% after 30 years of decline.[2]
This increased interest in locating production in the U.S. is
largely attributable to the fact that many companies are now
accounting for more than just labor costs, and are increasingly
using a total cost analysis when deciding where to manufacture. Some of the major reasons for re-shoring include: high
and increasing transportation costs, attractive domestic energy
prices, increased real estate and land costs in China, and increased hidden costs. Hidden costs include: product quality
control issues, complicated supply chains, logistics expenses,
longer development times, inability to accurately forecast rising costs (such as labor) due to uncertainty, and stolen intellectual property. Referring to the accuracy of forecast of future expenditures, U.S. manufacturers are the most productive
in the world, which has historically enabled unit labor costs
(ULCs) to stay relatively stable domestically, while many other
countries have volatile or increasing ULCs. These costs are not
easily captured in wage and productivity data, but companies
are increasingly trying to better account for them when making decisions on the best place to produce their products.

---

*The importance of simplifying the supply chain really
came to the forefront in 2011 after the Japanese tsunami
and the Thai floods, which made manufacturers rethink
just-in-time inventory management.*

Favorable energy prices have provided an additional tailwind to the re-shoring theme. Companies in highly energy in-
tensive industries are discovering that manufacturing in the
United States has become increasingly attractive. Industries set
to benefit most from these lower energy prices include: organic chemicals, resins, agricultural chemicals, petroleum re-

fining, metals (i.e., iron and steel), and machinery. This unconventional oil and natural gas boom has also put more money in consumer's pockets to spend on goods and services in the U.S.; some estimates have been as high as $324 billion in savings for the U.S. consumer in 2013.

As technology and automation drive an increasing share of the manufacturing process, labor costs share of the overall pie shrinks. Logistics and transportation costs can overpower labor advantages in some developing markets. The importance of simplifying the supply chain really came to the forefront in 2011 after the Japanese tsunami and the Thai floods, which made manufacturers rethink just-in-time inventory management. It also brought to light the vulnerability of complex supply chains where one or two small inputs from these countries delayed shipments of products made elsewhere. Another development is the demand for more customization by developed market consumers, resulting in manufacturers needing to produce in smaller order sizes. In China, high order minimums have made this difficult and it is a niche that U.S. manufacturers have been able to capitalize on. Intellectual property rights have also increased in importance as the Emerging Markets, particularly China, move up the value chain.

Job Growth

So what have been the impacts of these developments on labor thus far? Signs suggest that the U.S. labor market's demand for manufacturing personnel today is stronger than it has been in some time. Average weekly hours worked per production and nonsupervisory worker are at the highest level since the 1940s, and overtime hours are at historically elevated levels. . . . Wages are also beginning to show signs of life in the manufacturing sector . . . , though some industries are seeing stronger wage growth than others.

Manufacturing's unemployment rate hit the lowest level since 2008 in April at 5.2%, and durable goods manufacturing came in even lower at 4.6%. Some industries within manufacturing are seeing unemployment for those with prior industry work experience at rates below 3%. This data indicates that manufacturing companies are operating near full capacity on the labor front. This may lead to increased hiring activities assuming they can find people with the necessary skills to fill the job openings, and wages may begin to rise at a faster pace. Manufacturing jobs tend to be attractive from an earnings perspective, as the compensation per hour worked exceeds that of the average job.

As mentioned in our initial overview on the Manufacturing Renaissance, there are also multiplier effects when manufacturing and energy jobs are created. . . . Manufacturing states have shown an overall strength in payroll growth not seen in non-manufacturing states.[3] According to manufacturing.gov, the employment multiplier effect is 1.6 additional local service jobs for every 1 job created in manufacturing; however, this multiplier varies by industry, and in high-tech manufacturing, the multiplier can be as high as creating 5 local service jobs for every 1 manufacturing job. Furthermore, the amount of research & development will also increase as manufacturing comes back, as new research centers are set up like the General Electric global research center, which planned to hire 600 highly paid software engineers, data scientists, and user experience designers through the end of 2013.[4] The multiplier also helps the economies of the states beyond simply employment growth. According to the Bureau of Economic Analysis (BEA), manufacturing contributes $1.35 in additional economic activity for every $1 it spends. This is the highest multiplier of any major economic activity based on the BEA's methodology.

Where Do We Go from Here?

The improvement in American manufacturing appears to be sustainable and the potential for further growth from here remains a strong possibility. Favorable conditions which could foster further growth going forward are: stable/lower domestic energy prices, potential for increased demand for greater capital investment, volatility in international shipping costs, and rising or unpredictable ULCs in the Emerging Markets. However, nearly all of the threats and challenges that we identified back in 2012 remain true today.

Tight manufacturing labor capacity has lead to increased wages and more overtime for workers.

Capacity utilization rates in both the manufacturing sector and the broader economy are running at post-recession highs and in line with 30 year historical averages. At the same time spare capacity has declined, the average age of plant and equipment has reached new highs. This will make these companies more likely to replace these older, and likely less efficient, machines to increase productivity. The Business Round Table CEO [chief executive officer] Survey showed a renewed strength in plans for capital spending in March [2014], indicating some willingness to invest as demand increases. Increased appetite for capital spending should in turn lead to additional manufacturing activity to produce the needed equipment.

Another leg of the capital spending story is energy as a source of demand. Oil technological advances have helped bring new supply to market, but the reality is that global oil supply has been "running to stand still" for some time now. As oil wells age, their level of output generally declines, requiring additional wells and equipment in order to maintain the oil field's output. This is good news for U.S. Manufacturing in terms of equipment demand. Capital spending has grown at double digits for most of the past 13 years, yet OPEC [Organization of the Petroleum Exporting Countries] excess capacity has actually declined since 2000.

Although additional capital spending is likely, we caution against becoming too optimistic on this front. After all, in a slow growth world, how much capital spending is really necessary to keep up with demand growth? If companies are unsure about future economic growth, they are likely to continue squeezing as many years as they can out of their current equipment. Furthermore, although capacity utilization is nearing its 30 year historical average, prior to the 1980s, the economy ran at much tighter capacity on average, suggesting that there may still be further room to grow before greater capital spending is required.

Labor force dynamics remain one of the more significant headwinds to the Manufacturing Renaissance today. Tight manufacturing labor capacity has lead to increased wages and more overtime for workers. Although wage growth is a positive for the consumer, if wages rise too quickly, it may be sufficient to diminish the all-in attractiveness of manufacturing in the U.S. Equally important is the fact that the workforce continues to age in many industries such that there is a risk of net decline in workers as Baby Boomers continue to retire. Hundreds of thousands of jobs remain unfilled in manufacturing and other skilled labor industries because the current workforce doesn't have the adequate skills to fill these positions. The upshot is that the U.S. has access to a more highly skilled workforce than many economies and the demographic backdrop looks to be a greater challenge for many developed nations outside the U.S. While this creates a relative advantage of sorts for the U.S., many European countries are further ahead in setting up apprenticeship programs to bridge this gap. According to the U.S. Labor Department, formal programs combining on-the-job learning with mentorships and classroom education have declined 40% over the past decade. The good news on this front is that recently these training programs have begun to expand once again.

Finally, there are many policy risks that could threaten the sustainability of the recent gains in domestic manufacturing.

While protectionism has been a relatively benign concern of late, it does bear close monitoring. Any moves towards greater protectionist policies and trade restrictions will likely have negative repercussions on the manufacturing sector. Additionally, tax policy is another factor that can influence decisions as to where a company will locate various business activities. The individual tax rate is also very important to manufacturers, as two-thirds of manufacturers are flow-through entities and pay taxes at individual tax rates. Rather than trying to predict policy changes, it is more important to monitor risks such as these and update our outlook accordingly.

Slow Growth

The title of our 2012 exploration of the Manufacturing Renaissance—*Silver Lining, Not Silver Bullet*—continues to describe our view on the topic. The outlook for U.S. manufacturing continues to improve, and for the past two years it has been a positive contributor to overall economic activity. The resurgence of domestic energy production, rising labor costs in the developing world, increased transportation costs, and the emergence of more training programs for skilled workers are all positives for this theme. However, headwinds such as rising U.S. labor costs, the skills gap, government and regulatory hurdles, and lackluster global growth are sufficient to dictate restraint when forming expectations for future growth. At present, we believe that the ongoing evolution of this theme will create opportunities for select companies and industries, but it is not a big enough tailwind yet to change our overall slow growth outlook. We will continue to closely monitor this topic and provide additional updates as conditions warrant.

Notes

1. Celasun, Oya, Gabriel Di Bella, Tim Mahedy, and Chris Papageorgiou. "The U.S. Manufacturing Recovery: Uptick or Renaissance?" International Monetary Fund. February 2014. Web. <https://www.imf.org/external/pubs/ft/wp/2014/wp1428.pdf>

2. Ibid.

3. Manufacturing States are defined here as all states which derived 20% or more of their GDP from private-goods producing industries.

4. Roroohar, Rana, and Bill Saporito. "Made in the USA." *Time*. April 22, 2013. Web. <http://business.time.com /made-in-the-u-s-a>

The Manufacturing Resurgence Will Not Solve the Unemployment Crisis

Richard Florida

Richard Florida is cofounder and editor-at-large of CityLab.com and senior editor at The Atlantic.

While manufacturing is making a comeback in the United States, there has not been a large resurgence in the number of manufacturing jobs. Increased productivity through enhanced technology and the use of robotics will mean that fewer workers are needed to operate modern facilities. Furthermore, the manufacturing jobs that are being created are not much different in compensation than those in the food service and retail industries. Rather than trying to rebuild the manufacturing sector, the United States should focus more on driving innovation and transforming low-wage jobs into higher-paying ones.

In last night's [February 12, 2013] State of the Union address, President [Barack] Obama said: "Our first priority is making America a magnet for new jobs and manufacturing." He added:

> After shedding jobs for more than 10 years, our manufacturers have added about 500,000 jobs over the past three. Caterpillar is bringing jobs back from Japan. Ford is bringing jobs back from Mexico. After locating plants in other

countries like China, Intel is opening its most advanced plant right here at home. And this year, Apple will start making Macs in America again.

Manufacturing Is Insufficient

While there is much to applaud about the recent revival of American industry, manufacturing is simply insufficient to help revive lagging industrial regions or power the job creation the nation so badly needs. Here's why:

1. Manufacturing does not generate a lot of jobs: American manufacturing is making a comeback, but it remains an anemic job creator. Manufacturing output is projected to grow from $4.4 trillion in 2010 to a projected $5.7 trillion by 2020, according to the Bureau of Labor Statistics [BLS]. But this increased manufacturing output—which stems from improvements in technology, greater use of robots and automation, and improved production organization—will not necessarily translate into a whole lot more jobs. In fact, the BLS projects the U.S. will lose another 73,100 manufacturing jobs by 2020, as manufacturing falls to just seven percent of total employment.

Many manufacturing jobs that are being brought back onshore offer substantially lower wages than existing manufacturing jobs.

2. Not all manufacturing jobs are good jobs: Americans often think of manufacturing jobs as good, family-supporting union jobs, but unfortunately that's not actually the case. Production workers across the United States average just $34,220 per year according to the BLS, less than half that of knowledge, professional and creative workers ($70,890) and not that much more than what low skill service workers in fields like food preparation, clerical work and retail sales ($30,597) take

home. Pay varies considerably across different types of manufacturing jobs. As I noted here last March [2012]:

> The 66,530 tool and die makers or the 36,200 aircraft assemblers have great jobs earning—$48,710 and $45,230, respectively. But the nearly 150,000 sewing machine operators average just $22,630 a year, or $10.88 per hour.

While we like to think manufacturing jobs are secure, they are actually among the most vulnerable to the ups and downs of the business cycle. As I noted on *Cities* this past October [2012], the unemployment rate for workers in blue-collar jobs increased to 14.6 percent during the economic crisis, more than three times the rate of 4.1 percent for knowledge, professional, and creative workers, and considerably higher than the 9.3 percent rate for workers in low-skill service jobs which we typically think of as more vulnerable.

Also, many manufacturing jobs that are being brought back onshore offer substantially lower wages than existing manufacturing jobs. "U.S. manufacturing wages have come under further pressure as large established companies like General Electric, Ford and others have instituted two-tier pay practices," I wrote on *Cities* last year based on a report by the *New York Times*, which found new hires making just $12 to $19 per hour compared to $21 to $32 per hour for established employees.

3. Manufacturing jobs are concentrated in only some parts of the country: According to a recent Cleveland Fed [Federal Reserve Bank of Cleveland] study, manufacturing remains massively concentrated in the United States. Manufacturing makes up an 11 percent share of U.S. employment. But the distribution of manufacturing employment in the U.S. is highly skewed. As the report notes:

> The top 25 percent of counties in terms of their share of manufacturing employment derive about 18 percent or more of their employment from manufacturing. While these coun-

ties contain about one-fourth of the manufacturing employment in the United States, they contain only one-eighth of
the U.S. population.

Manufacturing jobs are overwhelmingly concentrated in
the middle of the country, not just in the industrial Midwest
but in adjacent parts of the Sun Belt, especially along Inter-
state 75 in the states of Kentucky down to Georgia, forming a
southern industrial heartland. There are only a few red spots
in the West.

The study finds that while high-manufacturing-share
counties did rebound during the economic recovery, in the
"last year or two employment growth has been roughly the
same in the high-manufacturing-share counties as it has been
in the rest of the country." . . .

---

*When all is said and done, it's not manufacturing that
drives economic growth and creates new jobs, but innovation, creativity and talent.*

Employment in high-manufacturing counties experienced
a five percent decline, employment in the rest of the nation's
counties increased by five percent "revealing a stark diver-
gence," according the report.

The findings from the Cleveland Fed's report are in line
with two related studies by Bill Testa of the Chicago Fed [Fed-
eral Reserve Bank of Chicago], which found the heavy con-
centration of manufacturing in the Midwest actually hindered
the economic development of its cities and metros (I wrote
about this study last year [2012] on *Cities*). Testa's detailed research concluded that "even after accounting for the influence
of educational attainment, a historical manufacturing orienta-
tion tended to depress subsequent growth"—an effect which
was felt for the better part of two decades. As *Cities* contributor Micheline Maynard pointed out last year, betting on

manufacturing's revival is likely to be a "big economic miscalculation" for Midwest cities, ultimately doing "more harm than good."

Creating New Jobs for the Future

President Obama should know better. It's time for our leaders to stop looking backward, trying to breathe life back into an economy that no longer exists, and develop an economic and job's strategy for the one that actually exists and will shape our future.

When all is said and done, it's not manufacturing that drives economic growth and creates new jobs, but innovation, creativity and talent. The big job generators for the past several decades and for the foreseeable future remain high-skill, high-pay knowledge jobs and low-pay, low-skill service jobs. We need to leverage and deepen the former, investing in the knowledge, technology and skill that drive innovation and economic growth. At the same time, we need to transform the more than 60 million low-wage service jobs into good family-supporting jobs like manufacturing jobs used to be.

That's the State of the Union we're still waiting to hear.

5

Manufacturing Jobs Can Support a New Generation of Workers

Pamela M. Prah

Pamela M. Prah is a political editor at Stateline.org.

There are many opportunities for those interested in manufacturing to obtain a high-paying, high-tech job. The manufacturing sector is targeting high school and college students and working to change the perception that manufacturing jobs resemble those of years past. There is an excellent future ahead for manufacturing in the United States and for the employees who take advantage of the career possibilities in the manufacturing sector.

Manufacturers across the United States are targeting schools and colleges to let young people know there is more to manufacturing than pulling levers on an assembly line.

"People still have the idea that manufacturing is a dirty dungeon place," said Andy Bushmaker of KI Furniture, a maker of school desks and cafeteria tables in Green Bay, Wisconsin. The goal, Bushmaker said, is to get people to see manufacturing jobs as the high-tech, high-skilled and high-paying careers they can be in the second decade of the 21st century.

Today's manufacturers, whether they are making cars, airplanes, or iPhone parts, are looking for engineers, designers, machinists and computer programmers. Manufacturing has moved from manual mills and lathes to computerized numerical control equipment and 3-D printers. Hand-held welders are being replaced with robotic welders. Industrial maintenance mechanics no longer need to know how to use a wrench, but have to be able to operate a "programmable logic control," or a digital computer, to fix the machines.

Many of the jobs pay well—the average manufacturing worker in the United States earned $77,505 in 2012, including pay and benefits—but they can be hard to fill.

Not Enough Workers

Nationwide, U.S. employers reported last year that skilled trades positions were the most difficult to fill, the fourth consecutive year this job has topped the list, according to the 2013 Manpower Group talent shortage survey. A 2011 industry report estimated that as many as 600,000 manufacturing jobs were vacant that year because employers couldn't find the skilled workers to fill them, including machinists, distributors, technicians and industrial engineers.

Wisconsin is one of many states where employers, schools and chambers of commerce are working together—often with the help of state or federal grant money—to prepare students and the unemployed for hard-to-fill manufacturing jobs. In Wisconsin, manufacturers figure they will have to fill 700,000 vacancies over the next eight years because of retirements. Employers like KI Furniture are using an array of programs to attract people to fill the pipeline, including youth and adult apprenticeships, job training, even YouTube videos. KI's own video includes an automation specialist who describes his work as, "the CSI [crime scene investigation] of the automation world."

Elsewhere:

- Teams of high school students in northeast Ohio get to design and build their own working robots with help from manufacturing companies as part of a "RoboBots" competition sponsored by Alliance for Working Together, a coalition of manufacturing companies. It has partnered with Lakeland Community College to develop a degree program working with an area high school to introduce an apprenticeship program starting in ninth grade.

- In Massachusetts, Siemens, the global industrial giant, announced last month [April 2014] it would donate nearly $660 million in software to a dozen technical schools and colleges in Massachusetts to help train a new generation of workers in advanced manufacturing.

- In Pittsburgh, the Three Rivers Workforce Investment Board teamed up with Carnegie Mellon [University], local community colleges, unions and apprenticeship programs to develop a "virtual hiring hall" for advanced manufacturing under a $3 million federal "innovation" grant.

[In 2012] the U.S. Labor Department announced it would provide $500 million to community colleges and universities around the country for innovative training programs.

Industry leaders in Kansas, Georgia, Rhode Island and Delaware this month [May 2014] joined the "Dream It. Do It." campaign started by the Manufacturing Institute, an affiliate of the National Association of Manufacturers. The goal of the program, which now has participants in 29 states, is to recruit students into manufacturing by educating parents, teachers and counselors about employment opportunities.

Recruiting the Next Generation of Workers

KI Furniture finds many of its future workers through involvement with the NEW (North East Wisconsin) Manufacturing Alliance, which consists of manufacturers, schools, chambers of commerce and workforce development boards. The members work together to promote manufacturing careers, particularly to young people.

"It's critical for us to continue to promote manufacturing careers as more and more retirements happen," Bushmaker said.

The NEW Manufacturing Alliance has received about $200,000 in state workforce development training grants over the last eight years, including $40,000 from Republican Gov. Scott Walker's Fast Forward grant program. The alliance has partnered with Northeast Wisconsin Technical College, which received $15 million in federal funds in 2012, when the U.S. Labor Department announced it would provide $500 million to community colleges and universities around the country for innovative training programs.

> *Students [in Wisconsin] who learn in the "Computer Integrated Manufacturing Mobile Lab" can earn college credits.*

Manufacturing remains an important part of the Wisconsin economy. More than 16% of Wisconsin workers are in manufacturing, more than any other state save Indiana, the National Association of Manufacturers reported in 2013. In northeast Wisconsin, manufacturing makes up 23% of all jobs.

Every year the NEW Manufacturing Alliance surveys its members to see which jobs are hard to fill and then teams up with local high schools and the Northeast Wisconsin Technical School to come up with ways to encourage students in those careers, providing classes and a pathway to those jobs.

Welding, for example, used to be one of the most difficult jobs to fill. Only 28 welders graduated from the Northeast Wisconsin Technical School in 2005. But five years later, that number jumped to 109 graduates. Today, 180 welders are enrolled in the program and welding has dropped to No. 8 among the hard-to-fill jobs, said Ann Franz, director of the NEW Manufacturing Alliance.

Skilled machinist jobs are now the hardest to fill in northeast Wisconsin. Enter a roving 44-foot trailer and truck equipped with computer numerical control, manufacturing tools and 12 work stations that travels to rural school districts to provide students with hands-on training. Students who learn in the "Computer Integrated Manufacturing Mobile Lab" can earn college credits.

The alliance also has produced videos that local teachers use to teach practical applications for math on a production line—from trigonometry to software optimization to robotics. And this fall, the NEW Manufacturing Alliance is working with the Green Bay Area School District and Northeast Wisconsin Technical College to launch a new lab located at West High School called Bay Link Manufacturing that will give high school students in the Green Bay area "real world projects" from local manufacturing companies, allowing them to use computerized numerical control manufacturing tools.

Network of "Manufacturing Hubs"

President [Barack] Obama wants to build a network of "manufacturing hubs" to bring together companies, universities and other academic and training institutions to develop the latest manufacturing techniques. The president announced in February [2014] a new public-private partnership near Detroit [Michigan] devoted to developing new types of light weight metals and another in Chicago [Illinois] to concentrate on digital manufacturing and design technologies.

Manufacturing hubs already have been established in Youngstown, Ohio, and Raleigh, North Carolina. The initiatives use money from the U.S. Defense and Energy departments that is already budgeted, since Congress has balked at the president's $1 billion price tag for the hubs.

As part of this effort, employers such as Dow, Alcoa, and Siemens are partnering with community colleges in Northern California and South Texas on apprenticeships in advanced manufacturing occupations, such as welding. In Minnesota, a coalition of 24 community colleges, led by South Central College, is pioneering a statewide apprenticeship model in mechatronics.

Last month, the Obama administration announced $100 million in federal grants for creating or expanding apprenticeship programs. At the state level, Rhode Island this week [May 2014] enacted the state's first registered manufacturing apprenticeship program while last year Connecticut increased the manufacturing apprenticeship tax credit to $7,500 from $4,800.

Apprenticeships are "underappreciated and underutilized," according to U.S. Secretary of Labor Thomas E. Perez. Perez said that when he hears a parent say, "I don't want my kid to do an apprenticeship; I want my kid to go to college," he points to the program at Tampa Electric in Florida, which pays apprentices about $32 an hour as they learn how to maintain and repair electrical power systems and equipment. They can earn as much as $70,000 as full-time employees. "Some of the upper management at Tampa Electric started out as lines people," Perez said.

"There is a bright future in America for people who work with their hands," Perez said. "We need to do a better job of marketing it, explaining to parents and others that these jobs are tickets to the middle class."

6

US Workers Are Competitive in the Global Manufacturing Marketplace

The Executive Office of the President and the Department of Commerce

The Executive Office of the President is a group of federal entities led by staff who work directly with the President of the United States. The Department of Commerce is the US federal agency within the executive office that directs and promotes domestic and international finance.

The United States has a competitive advantage in the global marketplace. The reasons are numerous but include the skilled and highly productive American workforce, access to patents for goods and intellectual property, inexpensive energy, and easier access to markets. As a result, numerous foreign companies are choosing to relocate their operations to the United States, and many US firms are bringing manufacturing jobs back to the country from abroad. This has resulted in thousands of new jobs for Americans across many industries.

The United States is highly competitive globally as a destination for investment. In AT Kearney's 2013 FDI [Foreign Direct Investment] Confidence Index, the United States surged past countries like China, Brazil and India to become the country with the top FDI prospects globally, as ranked by 302

"Winning Business Investment in the United States," The Executive Office of the President, The Department of Commerce, May 2014.

companies representing 28 countries and multiple industry sectors. This marks the first time that the United States occupied the #1 spot in the survey since 2001.

The United States' Competitive Advantages

A number of growing advantages make the United States a winning destination for investment including:

- One of the most highly skilled and productive workforces in the world

- Global leadership in innovation and invention

- A booming energy sector and low-cost natural gas and electricity

- Rapid access to domestic and global markets

Businesses are waking up to value of the United States' competitive advantages, even over low-wage locations. In the past, low wages and cost competitiveness were considered synonymous, with businesses "chasing low wages" in making decisions about where to invest, regardless of skill and productivity differences between the low-wage and American workforces. However, experience in low-wage countries has imparted a more nuanced view. Businesses have learned that today's low wages may be gone tomorrow and that other costs and risks often offset the savings from cheap labor. As a result, more businesses are taking a fresh look at the advantages the United States holds for investment.

In 2013, the World Bank ranked the United States fourth out of 185 countries in terms of the "ease of doing business."

A Skilled and Highly Productive Workforce. The U.S. workforce is among the most highly skilled and innovative in the world. The United Nations Development Program ranks the

United States first in the world in average years of schooling, a global measure for richness of human capital. The United States' strong education and training system including high schools, community colleges and four-year institutions provides a national infrastructure for job-driven training and has been strengthened by Administration efforts, including a fresh infusion of more than $2 billion, to ensure the availability of skilled workers for all firms operating in the United States. Not surprisingly given its high degree of skills, the U.S. workforce is among the most productive in the world—more than 30 percent more productive than Germany's and nearly twice as productive as South Korea's workforce. And the U.S. workforce is set to maintain this significant advantage thanks to ongoing productivity growth.

The International Energy Agency estimates that in 2012 alone, lower gas and electricity prices in the United States versus Europe saved the U.S. manufacturing industry close to $130 billion.

Global Leadership in Innovation. The United States is the world's leading source of innovation and invention. Fifteen of the top 25 research universities in the world and many more top-flight research institutions are located in the United States. These universities and institutions are essential partners for companies making R&D [research and development] investments here like GLOBALFOUNDRIES, which located a $2 billion Technology Development Center in upstate New York in part to access nearby research partnerships. The United States ranks among the top five on the World Intellectual Property Organization's rankings in both investment in knowledge as a share of GDP [gross domestic product] and in innovation. 33.8 percent of world R&D investments are made in the

United States. Moreover, the United States retains its lead as the world's most inventive country in 2013, accounting for 27.9 percent of all international patent applications among 148 nations.

And companies locating in the United States for access to innovation can rest assured that their investments in research and their discoveries will be protected through our strong and accessible system for intellectual property protection. Government fees for obtaining a U.S. patent are among the lowest in the industrialized world and discounted fees are available for small and medium sized entities. While there is still more that we need to do to ensure that our patent system creates the right incentives to encourage innovation and invention, this intellectual property regime is just one example of the stable and predictable regulatory environment that the United States has to offer. A predictable regulatory environment, in turn, makes doing business easier. In 2013, the World Bank ranked the United States fourth out of 185 countries in terms of the "ease of doing business."

Booming Energy Sector. Increased domestic energy production has brought down prices and brightened the U.S. energy outlook, most notably for natural gas. Between 2007 and 2012, U.S. prices for natural gas dropped nearly 60 percent as production rose and new reserves were uncovered. In contrast, the northern European or Asian spot markets post prices ranging from twice to several times the prices paid in the United States. The country's natural gas boom has catalyzed domestic and foreign investment in petrochemical manufacturing as well as in the manufacturing of steel and equipment needed for gas extraction. Indeed petrochemical companies have announced over $80 billion of planned investments in the United States, taking advantage of this low-cost energy and feedstocks. Multiple industries benefit directly from inexpensive U.S.-produced natural gas because of its diverse industrial uses, ranging from on-site electricity generation to process heating, space heating, steam generation, and petro-chemical processing. The International Energy Agency esti-mates that in 2012 alone, lower gas and electricity prices in the United States versus Europe saved the U.S. manufacturing industry close to $130 billion.

The United States . . . has free trade agreements in place with 20 countries and a host of bilateral investment trea-ties that promote exports.

In addition, rapidly growing domestic demand for renew-able energy offers opportunities for firms to produce in the United States to serve this demand and to offset high shipping costs for heavy parts such as wind turbine towers and blades. Since 2008, the amount of solar power installed in the U.S. has increased nearly 11-fold, to an estimated 13 gigawatts. 72 percent of wind turbine components installed in the United States in 2012, such as towers, blades, and gears, were made in America, nearly tripling the 25 percent domestic share in 2006–2007.

Access to Domestic and Global Markets. A recent study finds that access to markets is one of the factors driving the deci-sions of multinationals to locate in the United States. The U.S. economy is the largest in the world, and with a median house-hold income of $51,371 in 2012, offers a large and steady de-mand for a variety of products. A policy of "build where you sell" allows firms to gain deep insight into how local consum-ers use a firm's product, uses that may differ significantly from those in a multinational's home market. And locating in the United States to serve U.S. demand allows companies to react quickly to increased data on demand to get ahead of the com-petition, while also avoiding dozens of hidden costs. Examples of such costs include the long trips and time of top executives required to communicate with suppliers abroad, risk associated with uncertainty in shipping prices and delivery times and difficulty in verifying product quality over long supply chains.

While we have more to do to keep pace with other countries when it comes to investing in our infrastructure, the United States possesses a legacy of world-class ports plus freight rail, air transportation, and road networks capable of not only serving the large U.S. market but making the United States a base for exports as well. U.S. regulations for exporting are also among the easiest in the world. Specifically, the United States requires the least amount of time to comply with all procedures for exporting goods among 185 countries surveyed by the World Bank. The United States also has free trade agreements in place with 20 countries and a host of bilateral investment treaties that promote exports. And the Administration is working to open up additional markets to U.S. exports through trade agreements that are on the way. U.S. affiliates of foreign firms take advantage of this access to global markets—accounting for a significant share of total U.S. exports. For example, in 2011, U.S. affiliates of foreign firms exported $303.7 billion of goods, accounting for 20.5 percent of total U.S. goods exports, the second highest share since 1995.

The United States consistently ranks as one of the top destinations in the world for investment and has been the largest recipient of foreign direct investment since 2006.

Businesses Are Increasing Investment in the United States

Recent studies have demonstrated that global businesses see the United States as an increasingly competitive place in which to invest. The Organization for International Investment

(OFII) and PricewaterhouseCoopers LLP (PwC) recently presented findings from their 2014 Insourcing Survey, showing significant confidence in the United States as a location for companies and supply chains. The survey showed that 51 percent of global companies with U.S. operations plan to increase U.S. employment in 2014 and 64 percent plan to increase their investment in the United States this year.

The Boston Consulting Group (BCG) in a 2013 survey similarly found that more than half (54 percent) of executives at U.S.-based manufacturing companies with sales greater than $1 billion are considering re-shoring production to the United States—up from 37 percent in 2012. BCG further found a doubling since 2012 in the share of U.S.-based executives who are actively shifting production from China to the United States.

The attractiveness of the United States for investment is also evidenced by the fact that the United States consistently ranks as one of the top destinations in the world for investment and has been the largest recipient of foreign direct investment since 2006, with investment inflows totaling more than $1.5 trillion through 2012. And more recently, the United States has experienced a steep change in its share of foreign direct investment inflows to developed countries—with half of all inflows to G7 countries destined for the United States. [G7 is a group of seven nations with the most advanced economies in the world.]

These investments further strengthen the U.S. economy: they support well-paying jobs for millions of U.S. workers, expand our exports, and fund research and development.

Foreign Direct Investment in the United States Is Substantial. Precise data on the amount of investment U.S. firms have returned to the U.S. from abroad, or kept in the U.S., are difficult to assess, but investment by foreign firms into the United States, an easier-to-quantify proxy for the United States overall competitiveness is substantial and growing.

- In 2013, net U.S. assets of foreign affiliates totaled $4.6 trillion and FDI inflows totaled $193 billion.

- In 2012, the U.S. manufacturing sector accounted for approximately 50 percent of the total share of FDI dollars flowing into the United States, led by pharmaceuticals and petroleum and coal products. Outside manufacturing, wholesale trade accounted for 12 percent, while mining, non-bank holding companies, finance and insurance, and banking accounted for the bulk of the remaining 38 percent of total foreign investment.

- Since 2010, Japan, Canada, Australia, Korea, and seven European countries collectively have accounted for more than 80 percent of new FDI into the United States. Although still small, investment flows from emerging economies are growing rapidly.

- Since 2010, the United States has experienced a steep change in its share of FDI inflows to developed countries, as measured by inflows to the G7, receiving a nearly 50 percent share of total FDI inflows to developed countries annually. More than two-thirds higher than its typical share of developed country FDI inflows in prior years.

Whatever the form, [foreign direct investment] ultimately translates into output, jobs, exports, R&D, and growth of the U.S. economy.

Global Investment Benefits the U.S. Economy

As the President explained, fostering strong demand and a productive business environment in turn attracts investment, together contributing to strong economic performance. Business investment is a key source of capital, employment, innovation, and cross-border trade. In the United States, business investments have led to the creation of competitive jobs, investments in fixed assets and research and development, and overall growth and innovation that drives U.S. competitiveness.

Since President Obama's Knox College speech [July 24, 2013], the number of private sector jobs has increased by nearly 1.8 million, making the total number of jobs over the past 50 months 9.2 million private sector jobs—with 647,000 in our nation's factories. Business investment has also been robust. In 2013, business fixed investment, measured as nonresidential fixed investment, totaled over $2 trillion and accounted for more than 20 percent of the rebound in real GDP since mid-2009.

Foreign direct investment is a prominent feature of the U.S. economic landscape and further highlights the role of business investment in economic performance. Inbound direct investment funds a number of types of physical assets, including production plants, research and development (R&D) facilities, sales offices, warehouses, and service centers. It can take the form of a "greenfield" establishment that creates new operations or a merger or acquisition ("M&A") of a sufficiently large stake in an existing enterprise. Whatever the form, it ultimately translates into output, jobs, exports, R&D, and growth of the U.S. economy.

Foreign companies investing in the United States created 120,000 manufacturing jobs between 2009 and 2011.

Global Investments Result in High-Paying Manufacturing Jobs. Global investment, as represented by majority-owned U.S. affiliates of foreign companies, creates high-paying U.S. jobs—because their employment is concentrated in high-skill occupations, compensation at U.S. affiliates of foreign companies has been consistently higher than the U.S. average and is true for both manufacturing and non-manufacturing jobs.

U.S. affiliates of foreign firms employed 5.6 million people in the United States, or 5.1 percent of private sector employment, in 2011. Consistent with estimates of the investment position by industry, about one-third of jobs at U.S. affiliates are in the manufacturing sector.

In 2011, manufacturing employment at U.S. affiliates of international firms was 2.1 million, or 17.8 percent of all U.S. manufacturing employment. Foreign companies investing in the United States created 120,000 manufacturing jobs between 2009 and 2011. And this trend has accelerated—one third of all manufacturing jobs created in 2011, the latest year for which we have data, were from foreign companies choosing to locate production here.

Next to manufacturing, the largest industry sectors for employment by U.S. affiliates are wholesale trade which employed 546,600 workers, representing 9.9 percent of total employment within the wholesale trade sector; retail trade with 488,500, representing 3.3 percent of total employment within the retail trade sector; and administration, support, and waste management with 482,200 workers, representing 6.2 percent of total employment within this sector.

Because global investment is concentrated in the knowledge-intensive, high-skilled industries in which the United States has a global edge, U.S. affiliates tend to hire highly skilled workers and pay excellent wages. These firms paid wages and other forms of compensation that averaged more than $77,000 per U.S. employee in 2011 as compared to average earnings of $58,000 for workers in the economy as a whole. Compensation at U.S. affiliates has been consistently higher than the U.S. average over time, and the differential holds for both manufacturing and non-manufacturing jobs, with a slightly higher differential in manufacturing.

Global Investment Punches Above its Weight in Output and R&D. In 2011, global investment, as measured by the activities of U.S. affiliates of foreign firms, accounted for only 4.7 percent of total U.S. private output, but contributed 9.6 percent of U.S. private investment and 15.9 percent of U.S. private research and development spending, more than nearly double and triple its respective share. U.S. affiliates are also well-integrated globally and are the source of 20.5 percent of total U.S. goods exports.

Global investment's share of U.S. research and investment is rising. In 2011, these firms spent $45.2 billion on R&D, accounting for 15.9 percent of total R&D spending by businesses. Since 1997, when the data were first published, R&D expenditures of U.S. affiliates have climbed 163 percent, close to double the 87 percent growth among overall business spending on R&D. The bulk of the R&D investments were in the manufacturing sector, which accounted for 69.9 percent of total R&D expenditures by U.S. affiliates. Affiliates in the wholesale trade sector spent $7.0 billion on R&D in 2011, followed by the professional, scientific, and technical services sector ($4.1 billion), and the information sector ($1.5 billion).

7

US Workers Are Not Competitive in the Global Manufacturing Marketplace

Willy C. Shih, interviewed by Harvard Magazine

Willy C. Shih is the Robert and Jane Cizik Professor of Management Practice in Business Administration at Harvard University. Harvard Magazine *is a publication of Harvard University that serves alumni, faculty, and students of the institution.*

The United States no longer has the expertise to design and build the components needed for modern products. This expertise was lost as US companies moved operations to other countries where labor was less expensive and policies more lax. Many people do not understand that manufacturing is quite sophisticated work, requiring engineers on the factory floors. With the loss of engineering expertise, it is difficult to grow the manufacturing sector in the United States.

*H*arvard Magazine: *You've had a lot of manufacturing experience.*

Willy Shih: I spent 28 years in industry. I confronted a lot of puzzles there, and I've been looking at them since coming here.

The interesting question relating to competitiveness had to do with my time at Kodak. In 1997, I took over the consumer digital business it was trying to build. That year Kodak shipped a few tens of thousands of digital cameras. One of the factories in Rochester, New York, had this highly automated assembly line where the engineers were attempting to manufacture digital cameras locally. You needed a whole bunch of electronic and optical components: electronic sensors, the tiny displays that show you your pictures, rechargeable batteries, consumer-electronic stuff.

I found that back in the 1960s and 1970s, all the money in photography was made manufacturing film. So Kodak let go of camera manufacturing except for the low-end, single-use cameras—basically just a box for film with a lens. In the same decades, U.S. consumer-electronics makers outsourced the assembly of TV sets to Asia, and then they gradually let go of more and more of the business.

The Loss of the American Advantage

So I arrive in Rochester and find that there is no more expertise in the U.S. for all the components you need to build a digital camera—not in LCD displays, electronic sensors, zoom lenses, or the tiny electric motors you need to drive zooms. There weren't people who made shutter buttons or view finders, or *any* of those components. So even though my team had decided we were going to be highly automated, you couldn't design and make digital cameras in the U.S. That was the first object lesson.

When your processes are not particularly mature, it really makes sense to be close to production.

That was repeated when I took over the organic LED (OLED) business. Kodak made the pioneering invention in organic electroluminescence. In solar photovoltaic cells, it's light in, electricity out; this is electricity in, light out. There are a lot of benefits to this technology; a Samsung Galaxy S smartphone has an OLED display. But the path to market required the ability to make extremely uniform, low-temperature polysilicon on glass. It was the same story: even though U.S. companies *invented* a lot of the technologies, they had given up on *commercializing* and manufacturing them, so there was no way for us to get to market in the U.S.

That led to my thinking about the similarity to the tragedy of the commons—the loss of the shared pastures in a town that nurtured all the farmers' animals. All these predecessor organizations had let these capabilities go because they didn't matter to them individually at the time—but they turned out to be critical if you wanted to go into some important *new* technologies. It raised the question: if you don't have capabilities in some of these areas, does that mean it no longer makes sense to invest in research and development and innovation in other new areas? Gary Pisano [Harvard Business School professor] and I pointed out in a 2009 *Harvard Business Review* article that you couldn't make an Amazon Kindle in the U.S. because many key capabilities no longer existed. The key technology in that device came out of MIT [Massachusetts Institute of Technology]: the electrophoretic beads for its e-paper display. It was commercialized by E Ink here in Cambridge [Massachusetts]. But they had to go to Asia to make the complete screen.

In a lot of manufacturing, a lot of value is created in commercialization and advanced manufacturing; a lot of that is sophisticated knowledge work.

What caused this dispersal of manufacturing?

When I grew up in the industry in the 1980s, the thing they always pounded into an engineer's head was the importance of product development and commercialization being close to production. When I was at IBM in Austin [Texas], our factory was across the road; when your processes are not particularly mature, it really makes sense to be close to production.

So why did everyone start outsourcing? When the Asian economy—specifically China—opened up, the labor-cost differential was so great and there was such a limitless supply, seemingly everybody focused on labor arbitrage. My fully loaded labor cost in Rochester in the late 1990s was more than 100 times higher than China's. Everybody just moved their manufacturing over there.

Now what happens if your engineers and designers have to be close to manufacturing? Well, we just fill the sky with planes. If you're on the product side of Apple, you spend a lot of time in China—near the factories, working out problems.

The core question is whether this affects your ability to innovate. Gary and I think there *is* an impact, especially in leading-edge technologies where manufacturing processes are not yet mature. So we've just called that out.

Part of the problem is that people don't think of manufacturing as *knowledge work*. They think of it as someone putting in four screws 2,400 times a day—and there is a lot of that in the more mature assembly areas. But in a lot of manufacturing, a lot of value is created in commercialization and advanced manufacturing; a lot of *that* is sophisticated knowledge work. If you wander around in factories around the world (since the beginning of 2011 I've been in more than a hundred factories), you see some very sophisticated knowledge work. In some of the advanced semiconductor fabrication lines in Asia, you have masters in engineering running production tools that cost as much as an airplane—$65 million, $70 million. They're extremely sophisticated and complex, and a lot of engineering goes on *on* the factory floor.

So one of the things we call out is that conception that manufacturing is not knowledge work. For some types of manufacturing, it is very important to maintain production capability because it's tied to your ability to innovate.

Building on Remaining Strength

Do you see a similar fate for some of the new industries American businesses have been counting on?

Photovoltaic panels are a problem because America has let go of a lot of the electronic supply chain and silicon-processing skills from semiconductors. The companies that manufactured semiconductors—that commons fed the flat-panel-display industry, the solar-panel industry, the energy-efficient lighting industry with LEDs, because a lot of the same capabilities flowed into those.

Singapore would love to be the biotech hub of the world: they are competing very aggressively for R&D and manufacturing facilities.

What about areas of U.S. strength like aerospace assembly, biotech, and medical devices—what are the risks there?

The same kinds of things. A couple of factors led to unquestioned U.S. manufacturing leadership at the end of the 1960s and early 1970s. We had institutional foundations and broad education in the practical arts, going back to the Morrill Land Grant Act. We controlled mass manufacturing going back to the nineteenth-century "American system of manufactures," with interchangeable parts and gauges, specialized tools, sequential productions—all leading to Henry Ford and mass assembly of automobiles. And at the end of World War II, all our competitors were in ruins. At the end of that war, we had this public perception that science had won the war—not just the atomic bomb, but things like radar, antibiotics, the proximity fuse, and countless other innovations. So as a country we had a lot of faith in science, and we invested heavily in our basic science and education.

But other countries did, too—Germany and Europe, but also Japan, the Asian tigers, and China. Now other countries compete very aggressively for those manufacturing facilities.

Singapore would love to be the biotech hub of the world: they are competing very aggressively for R&D [research and development] and manufacturing facilities. Every other Asian country is asking those questions as well: how do I capture more of these export-earning industries?

We haven't thought about preserving those types of capabilities. There are some industries where we're still pretty strong, like aerospace, especially jet engines—the engine manufacturers are pretty thoughtful about what is important to hold on to. But lots of other countries have decided what's important. In the capital-equipment businesses these days, if you're going to sell in a lot of countries, you need to provide production offsets for local manufacturers—so they begin picking up the skills and learn how to move to higher value-added.

Managers need to think longer term about those capabilities and about the context in which they're embedded.

I worry about composite materials, where the U.S. has really had a lead. We're shipping a lot of that overseas. I worry about biotech manufacturing and medical devices, where we have a lot of regulatory issues—Europe is a lot easier for medical devices, so we're chasing a lot of the companies that make them offshore.

It's a complex mix of factors, but again the key in my mind is preserving innovative capability. We talk about innovation a lot, but we don't recognize how important *making things* is to preserving some of that innovative capability over time.

Business and US Policy

What are the relative responsibilities of businesses and of policymakers in preserving those innovative capabilities?

Managers need to think longer term about those capabilities and about the context in which they're embedded. It's not only the people and knowledge within their walls—it's their supplier network and competitors in adjacent industries. Thinking about capabilities is key.

The government has to correct some of the policy deficits that caused the U.S. to be less favored as a location. Mike [Porter] and Jan [Rivkin]'s survey of HBS [Harvard Business School] alumni showed how few companies would actually choose to locate in the U.S. In some industries, location decisions are heavily influenced by tax incentives. But I can absolutely say that our complex tax law and relatively high rates of taxation motivate people to move operations offshore. So the government needs to think about how we at least get to a level playing field *and* it has the responsibility to invest in public goods: basic scientific research, education, and infrastructure—key parts of the "commons" that private companies are incapable of investing in.

What skills would the U.S. need to promote to tilt decisions about where to locate operations away from a strictly financial calculation about the cost of hiring suitable employees?

Once you allow those skills to dissipate, throw away those capabilities, a lot of those decisions are very expensive or impossible to reverse. My counsel is to be more thoughtful about that.

I just wrote a case on a large multinational that has its engineering center in India, with thousands of engineers and an average age of 27, and its home engineering operation in the U.S., where the average age is 47. The guys in India said the U.S. operations hadn't hired anybody in the past half-dozen years, so they don't have fresh skills. Do you retrain, or start with the younger generation and try to keep their skills fresh? That's a huge problem. I saw people at Kodak in film manufacturing who had amazing skills, but as technological substitution happens, those people can't take their skills anywhere.

The global market for tradable goods decimated the lower-skilled jobs. I think it's starting to attack highly skilled jobs, too. I don't have good answers, but I think that's the next huge issue.

8

The Focus on the Export of US Manufactured Goods Is Misguided

Derek Scissors, Charlotte Espinoza, and Terry Miller

Derek Scissors is senior research fellow in Asia economic policy in the Asian Studies Center at the Heritage Foundation. Charlotte Espinoza is a former research assistant in the Center for International Trade and Economics (CITE) at the Heritage Foundation. Terry Miller is a former US ambassador and is currently director of CITE at the Heritage Foundation.

Increased imports to the United States do not mean a loss of American jobs. To the contrary, as more goods are imported to the United States, more jobs are created in the fields of finance, wholesale and distribution, and transportation. Clothes and toys imported from China alone are estimated to be responsible for over half a million jobs in America. Policy makers should understand the importance of imports to the US economy and should support trade policies to increase both exports and imports.

Conventional wisdom says that exports are beneficial and imports are harmful. Conventional wisdom is wrong. A key element of this misperception is the mistaken idea that imports into a country cost jobs there. In fact, imports contribute to job creation.

Derek Scissors, Charlotte Espinoza, and Terry Miller, "Trade Freedom: How Imports Support US Jobs," The Heritage Foundation, September 9, 2012. Copyright © 2012 The Heritage Foundation. All rights reserved. Reproduced by permission.

In a political environment where trade and job creation are being hotly debated, it is vital to have a correct understanding of how imports truly affect jobs. The reality is that the increased economic activity associated with every stage of the import process helps support American jobs. A lot of them. The following analysis shows that over half a million American jobs are supported by imports of Chinese-made clothes and toys alone. These jobs are in fields such as transportation, wholesale, retail, construction, and finance, and in myriad other activities that are involved in turning a manufactured product into a good that is ready for use by the average American.

Imports Create Jobs

Imports from China of other products support additional jobs, as do imports from other countries. The belief that more imports equals less employment at home is false. It follows directly that the idea that trade deficits lead to higher unemployment is also false. Concern over the size of the U.S. trade deficit, and particularly its impact on jobs, is based on a misconception of the way trade affects economic activity.

Advocates of free trade have long established that imports provide choices that increase individual and national prosperity. These benefits do not come at the cost of employment— expanded economic activity due to trade in both directions *adds* jobs. Congress and the Administration should not be fooled by claims of jobs lost due to imports. The government can best bolster the U.S. economy, and increase employment, by moving away from protectionism and toward trade liberalization.

Trade and Employment in the Real World

According to the Census Bureau, the U.S. imported $382 billion of goods from China in 2010, almost one-fifth of total American imports that year. Some argue that huge volumes like this mean the U.S. has lost millions of jobs to China. There are different variations of this argument, and they are all fatally flawed. They (1) rely on misleading statistics, (2) misunderstand the crucial impact of choice and competition, and (3) confuse the impacts of recent trade with a single country (usually China) with the multi-generation process of globalization and improvements in productivity.

The competitive pressure from imports improves the quality of U.S. goods and services, further encouraging consumption.

The first flaw is with the trade data themselves. The way trade is almost always measured gives full credit to the country that sends the final shipment: The full value of a computer assembled in China counts as a Chinese export though, typically, the only part of the computer trade process that occurs in China is the manual assembly of the parts. The value added to China's economy is tiny, as are the workers' salaries. Yet China gets credit for the entire process in the trade accounts, and its export figures are very high.

This method of measurement ignores the fact that many imports into the U.S. start their lives as American intellectual property or components of goods, which are then modified or assembled overseas. The U.S. is a world leader in the creation of intellectual property, in product design, and in financing, and many final products imported into the U.S. contain parts originally manufactured in the U.S. High-quality American jobs are created in the early stages of what subsequently become import transactions, which are then wrongly said to lower net employment. That such activities create good jobs in the U.S. is universally accepted, but still often lost in policy discussions, which focus far too often on export promotion.

Protectionists do not advocate the use of faulty statistics. But they do have a faulty understanding of economics. The availability of more choices, usually at a lower price, in the form of imports allows American consumption to be higher than it otherwise would be. Even more important, the competitive pressure from imports improves the quality of U.S. goods and services, further encouraging consumption.

If China stopped exporting television sets, there would be fewer choices and less competition. The price of TVs would rise and the quality would fall. Americans would buy fewer TVs and production of TVs would then decline, in the U.S. and everywhere else. The ultimate logic of protectionism is to make everyone a loser.

The idea that millions of American jobs have been lost to China relies on bad trade numbers, bad economics, and a completely fictional view of the world.

Yet some criticism of free trade goes a step further. It wraps up all the effects of technological change and an increasingly integrated world economy and lays them at the feet of a trade deficit with one country. This was done in the 1970s and 1980s when Japan began to compete with the U.S. and Europe, leading some to see Japan as a villain. In fact, the increased competition spurred innovation and boosted productivity, and the U.S. and Europe were ultimately winners. Such economic change can cause short-term dislocations, particularly in the job market. But over the course of a few years, Japanese competition inspired a much healthier American economy, with more and better-paying jobs. Now that the Japanese economy has fallen on hard times and is no longer a convenient scapegoat, China has become the prime target of American protectionists.

Those who attack China often do not examine real economic events: They do not measure actual failed businesses and actual job losses. Instead, they assume the U.S.-China trade deficit means that both production and production jobs are moving from the U.S. to China. If this were true, many jobs would have moved back to the U.S. from China when the bilateral deficit fell by more than $30 billion in 2009. Of course, no jobs actually moved. Instead, millions of jobs were lost, due not to trade flows, but simply because of economic contraction during the financial crisis.

Even absent a crisis, the U.S.-China trade deficit does not have the impact on jobs that many protectionists believe it has. If the bilateral trade deficit were eliminated, jobs would not move to the U.S., because the U.S. does not trade with China alone. Furniture production and similar jobs would move from China, not to the U.S., but rather to other countries where furniture can be made cheaply. The idea that millions of American jobs have been lost to China relies on bad trade numbers, bad economics, and a completely fictional view of the world.

Imports and Jobs: The Real Relationship

It is easy to link exports to specific jobs. Government statistics that record the passage of products as they leave the country are easy to match with production and employment. The next step is to look at the impact on American employment of imported goods as they make their way from the port of entry to their final destination in homes, offices, or factories.

Protectionists frequently assume that the only impact of imports is to displace U.S. production. They ignore the market-expanding effect of the additional choices and competition brought by imports. Some protectionists also conveniently disregard activities that add value to a country's economy and that apply equally to imports and exports— such as port loading, internal transport, wholesale trade, retail trade, advertising, and after-market service. It is no help to policymaking to imagine what might happen if all goods Americans buy from China were suddenly produced here. This ignores the trade, investment, and business development that have contributed so much to American and world living standards. A more useful analysis embraces the world as it really works—in which imports undeniably support jobs.

The positive impact of imports on jobs can be seen clearly in the relationship over the past 30 years between the level of imports and the unemployment rate: When imports increase, the unemployment rate goes down, not up. One likely explanation for this phenomenon is that economic growth is driving both results—growth leads to more imports and simultaneously lowers unemployment. When growth collapses, as it did in 2009, imports weaken and unemployment rises. Imports do not cause unemployment; quite the opposite, they are a signal of prosperity and plentiful jobs.

The difference between the final price of goods to American consumers and the much lower value of those goods when they first entered U.S. territory is a measure of the value added in the U.S.

Further, it is possible to show how imports support jobs, and where. Examination of individual import categories shows that, rather than costing jobs, trade with China helps support hundreds of thousands of American jobs, at the very least. The figures are derived by calculating the value added to imports after they enter the U.S. and are unloaded, transported, and sold, then using that total to estimate the jobs being supported.

The results are clear and powerful. In 2010, imports of apparel from China helped support 355,000 American jobs. Toy and sporting goods imports helped support 221,000 jobs. The calculations were designed such that the bias is toward the downside, which means that these figures may well be too low. In just two trade categories, Chinese imports help support 576,000 jobs, and likely more.

The analytic concept is simple. The difference between the final price of goods to American consumers and the much lower value of those goods when they first entered U.S. territory is a measure of the value added in the U.S. Subtracting profits paid to capital investors leaves a figure representing the value added by American labor during this process. (Even fixed costs, such as for equipment, are ultimately separable into profit and value added for labor, so that some of the labor contribution is indirect.) Using average compensation for an individual worker, the result can be turned into an estimate of the number of American jobs being supported by all of the activities that occur between the port and the final users. This does not address all the important effects of imports as they expand consumer choices and affect the economy in many other ways, but can give an idea of the immediate impact of imports on jobs.

It makes little sense to focus on whether imports or exports are larger—whether there is a trade deficit or surplus—when both are having a positive impact.

The data requirements for this analysis turn out to be surprisingly tricky. While the data collected at port are for specific products, sales at the retail level are collected on the basis of the type of store, not the product. In concrete terms, the North American Industry Classification System (NAICS) for trade and output can be combined fairly precisely, but there is a sizable gap between these and the NAICS categories for sales.

Other valuable data sources, such as financial statements sent to the government, are imprecise about expenses or have important gaps, for example, with regard to port off-loading and transport. Notably, some data sources do not cover all goods. Bridging the gap between arrival at port and final sale is possible, however, with careful assessment of products and outlets.

A secondary challenge involves an estimate for profits. One problem: A single-year snapshot of profits can be misleading with regard to longer-term conditions as industry fortunes shift. While a considerable flaw in principle, it is easily addressed in practice. The procedure used allows simple substitution of different profit figures that will yield different numbers of jobs supported. When the profit figures used here become outdated, the same procedure can be used with new numbers.

Here, the procedure is applied to two industries—(1) clothing/apparel and (2) toys and sporting goods—in which imports from China are important in size and market share. The post-manufacturing and post-import supply chains for these products are thus very likely to be integrated, with domestic and foreign goods processed together. This allows measurements of total value added to be used in computing value added of goods specifically imported from China. . . .

Imports and Jobs in a New Light

The job-supporting nature of export production is intuitively obvious and captured in official reports and statistics. This is part of the reason why exports are considered to be good for the economy. Measuring the employment effects of imports is harder to do properly, but this is a start and much more progress can be made. Proper work in this area will continue to show that imports support jobs, too.

Because exports and imports both support jobs, it follows that the best measurement of how trade affects employment is the amount of combined trade flowing in and out of the country. It makes little sense to focus on whether imports or exports are larger—whether there is a trade deficit or surplus—when both are having a positive impact.

The Administration and Congress therefore should:

1. Recognize that imports support American jobs. Policymakers should resist legislation and regulations that restrict imports and adopt policies that encourage liberalization of trade in both directions.

2. Stop using the trade deficit to show the effect of trade on employment. Total trade volume is a far better indicator.

3. Improve trade data at a technical level. The Department of Commerce should measure components used in production, rather than just the final product. The Commerce Department and other agencies involved should also better align trade, production, and consumption classifications.

Understanding the positive role of imports in particular is critical to healthy trade policy and thus to bolstering the economy. Buying imports does not mean that jobs are exported to foreign nations. On the contrary, imports can create jobs from the port to the sales floor. The voluntary trade of dollars for goods is agreed upon millions of times every year because it benefits both parties to the transaction. American workers share intensely in those benefits.

9

US Trade Policy Sends Manufacturing Jobs Overseas

Daniel J. Ikenson

Daniel J. Ikenson is director of the Herbert A. Stiefel Center for Trade Policy Studies at the Cato Institute.

Manufacturing in the United States is suffering due to government regulations that make it more difficult to produce goods that require components built overseas. Imports are subject to fees that make the production of products that will later be exported or sold in the United States more expensive. It is essential that the government understand the relationship between imported goods and US manufacturing in order to support industries that rely on imports for the survival of their manufacturing operations. While many simplify the situation as "imports bad, exports good," the majority of imported goods are components or raw materials that the manufacturing sector needs in order to be successful.

Too many U.S. policymakers, from Capitol Hill to the various executive branch agencies in Washington [DC], tend to focus on foreign policies and foreign barriers when considering how best to improve the competitive prospects for U.S. firms. The presumption is that the major impediments to the success of U.S. firms are foreign born. Closed foreign markets, complex laws and regulations, overt flaunting of the trade rules, subtle protectionism, and unfair trade are the primary culprits that subvert the success of U.S. firms, discourage investment and hiring, and encourage offshoring of production. Indeed, that is the premise of today's hearing, as inferred from its description on the [US Congress Joint Economic] Committee's website.

But that premise is myopic and, frankly, irresponsible. It reinforces arguments for nonsensical policies, such as preserving our own barriers to trade and investment, which are nothing more than costs to U.S. businesses and families. Policies that raise the cost of doing business in the United States—such as our tariff regime and the industrial inputs—encourage manufacturers to at least consider moving operations abroad, where those materials are available at better prices.

Both parties to a trade are made better off. There are no losers, else the transaction wouldn't occur.

Governments are competing for business investment and talent, which both tend to flow to jurisdictions where the rule of law is clear and abided; where there is greater certainty to the business and political climate; where the specter of asset expropriation is negligible; where physical and administrative infrastructure is in good shape; where the local work force is productive; where there are limited physical, political, and administrative frictions. This global competition in policy is a positive development. But we are kidding ourselves if we think that the United States is somehow immune from this dynamic and does not have to compete and earn its share with good policies. The decisions made now with respect to our policies on immigration, education, energy, trade, entitlements, taxes, and the role of government in managing the economy will determine the health, competitiveness, and relative significance of the U.S. economy in the decades ahead.

Misleading the Public About Trade and Its Benefits

We live in a globalized economy where more and more U.S. jobs depend upon transnational collaboration—through integrated supply chains and cross-border investment. Most Americans enjoy the fruits of international trade and globalization every day: driving to work in vehicles containing at least some foreign content; communicating, shopping, navigating, and recreating on foreign-assembled smart phones; having higher disposable incomes because retailers like Wal-Mart, Best Buy, and Home Depot are able to pass on cost savings made possible by their own access to thousands of foreign producers; earning paychecks on account of their companies' growing sales to customers abroad; and enjoying salaries and benefits provided by employers that happen to be foreign-owned companies. Nearly 6 million Americans work for foreign subsidiaries in the United States.

Still, too many Americans are of the view that exports are good, imports are bad, the trade account is the scoreboard, the trade deficit means the United States is losing at trade, and it is losing because our trade partners cheat. Many point to the trade deficit as the obvious explanation for the much exaggerated death of U.S. manufacturing. According to polling data, Americans are generally skeptical about trade and its impact on jobs, manufacturing, and the U.S. economy. And come to think of it: why shouldn't they be? After all, the public is barraged routinely with misleading or simplistic coverage of trade issues by a media that is too often heavy on cliché, innuendo, and regurgitated conventional wisdom, and lacking in analytical substance or balance. And demagogic politicians only fan the flames of misconception and misgiving.

The [Barack] Obama administration has not been particularly helpful about correcting these misperceptions. In fact, the president is prone to using these scoreboard metaphors to describe trade, exhorting U.S. exporters to "win the future" or to secure foreign market share before other countries' firms get there or to beat the Chinese in developing this technology or that. This encouragement, with its incessant emphasis on exports as the benefits of trade and imports as its incidental costs, only reinforces the misconception that trade is a zero-sum game with distinct winners and losers. But trade does not lend itself to scoreboard metaphors because both parties to a trade are made better off. There are no losers, else the transaction wouldn't occur.

Policy Myopia

The centerpiece of the administration's almost indiscernible trade policy is the National Export Initiative [NEI], with its goal of doubling U.S. exports over five years (to $3.12 trillion by the end of 2014). That would be fine, except that nowhere in the administration's 68-page plan to double exports is the word "import" mentioned, except with respect to the section that speaks about strengthening the trade remedies laws to better discipline "unfair" imports. Some of the components of the NEI—such as streamlining U.S. export control procedures and concluding and signing trade agreements—are laudable ideas. But the plan is simply not good enough.

As currently executed, the NEI systemically neglects a broad swath of opportunities to facilitate exports by contemplating only the export-oriented activities of exporters. It presumes that U.S. exporters are born as exporters. But they are not. Before those companies are exporters, they are producers. And as producers, they are subject to a host of domestic laws, regulations, taxes, and other policies that handicap them in their competition for sales in the U.S. market and abroad.

According to a World Economic Forum survey of 13,000 business executives worldwide, there are 52 countries with less burdensome government regulations than those of the United States. Those regulations impose additional costs on U.S. businesses that sell domestically and abroad. As put by Andrew

Liveris, chairman and CEO [chief executive officer] of the Dow Chemical Company, "How we operate within our own borders, what we require of business here, often puts us at a competitive disadvantage internationally." By neglecting these domestic impediments, the administration pretends that the obstacles to U.S. competitiveness and export success are all foreign-born.

The policy reform focus must be broadened to include consideration of the full range of home grown policies—such as taxes, regulations, tariff policy, and contingent protectionism—that affect U.S. producers and put them at a disadvantage vis-á-vis foreign competitors.

Last year, U.S. Customs and Border Patrol collected $32 billion in duties on $2 trillion of imports, over $1 trillion of which were ingredients for U.S. production—such as chemicals, minerals and machine parts.

Obtaining Raw Materials from Overseas

As producers first, most U.S. exporters are consumers of capital equipment, raw materials, and other industrial inputs and components. Many of the inputs consumed by U.S. producers in their operations are imported or the costs of the inputs are affected by the availability and prices of imports. Indeed, "intermediate goods" and "capital equipment"—items purchased by producers, not consumers—accounted for more than 55 percent of the value of all U.S. imports last year [2010]—and 57 percent through the first half of 2011. That fact alone indicates that imports are crucial determinants of the profitability of U.S. producers and their capacity to compete at home and abroad. Yet the NEI commits not a single word to the task of eliminating or reducing the burdens of government policies that inflate import prices and production costs.

The president exhorts U.S. exporters to "win" a global race, yet he ignores the fact that the government's hodgepodge of rules and regulations has tied their shoes together.

If the administration were serious about helping U.S. companies become more competitive and making the NEI a long-lasting institution committed to U.S. international competitiveness, it would compile an exhaustive list of laws, regulations, policies, and practices that are undermining the stated objectives of increased competitiveness, economic growth, investment, and job creation through expanded trade opportunities.

Near the top of that list would be America's self-flagellating treatment of imported intermediate goods and other industrial inputs required by U.S. producers to make their final products. Last year [2010], U.S. Customs and Border Patrol collected $32 billion in duties on $2 trillion of imports, over $1 trillion of which were ingredients for U.S. production—such as chemicals, minerals and machine parts. Normal tariffs and special trade remedies duties (i.e., antidumping [AD, exporting a product for less than would be charged at home] and countervailing duties [CVD, import duties intended to counter subsidized goods in the global market]) added roughly $15-20 billion to the overall price tag, which would have been even higher had companies not been compelled to shutter domestic operations and, in some cases, relocate abroad on account of the higher input costs.

President Barack Obama understands this dynamic. Last year, when signing into law the Manufacturing Enhancement Act of 2010 (a bill to temporarily reduce or eliminate duties on certain imported raw materials) the president said:

The Manufacturing Enhancement Act of 2010 will create jobs, help American companies compete, and strengthen manufacturing as a key driver of our economic recovery. And here's how it works. To make their products, manufacturers—some of whom are represented here today—often have to import certain materials from other countries and pay tariffs on those materials. This legislation will reduce or eliminate some of those tariffs, which will significantly lower costs for American companies across the manufacturing landscape—from cars to chemicals; medical devices to sporting goods. And that will boost output, support good jobs here at home, and lower prices for American consumers.

Yet, the president's National Export Initiative contains provisions to "strengthen" the antidumping law, which will further frustrate domestic producers' access to imported inputs.

Antidumping Reform

The U.S. antidumping law still enjoys support in Congress and within pockets of the executive branch. Although some of that support can be chalked up to politicians representing the narrow interests of influential constituencies that have mastered the use of the antidumping and its highly misleading rhetoric, much more support stems from a fundamental misunderstanding of the purpose, history, mechanics, and consequences of the law.

Too many policymakers passively accept the anachronistic rationalizations proffered by the steel industry, labor unions, other big antidumping users, and their hired guns in Washington. Too many buy into the idealized imagery of a patriotic, upstanding American producer working tirelessly to ensure the preservation of well-paying jobs for hard-working Americans, but is suffering the ravages of unscrupulous, predatory foreign traders intent on destroying U.S. firms and monopolizing the U.S. market.

What politician could oppose a law presumed to protect that kind of a company against that kind of a scourge? But that is really a caricature, a myth. When the curtain is peeled back to expose the operation of the antidumping law, one can see a very different reality. Antidumping measures always raise the costs of firms in downstream industries that rely on the affected imports, and always claim domestic firms as victims. The law is often used as a tool by domestic firms waging battle for supremacy over other domestic firms, completely defying the foundational "us vs. them" premise upon which the AD status quo has come to rest. Sometimes foreign-owned firms are the petitioners and U.S-owned firms are the respondents. Rarely do antidumping restrictions lead to job creation or job restoration in the domestic industry, which is the most common claim of those seeking protection. And never is the allegation of "unfair trade" substantiated, or even investigated. Myth and misinformation explains the persistence of the U.S. antidumping regime.

Import-consuming producers suffer the costs and consequences of antidumping restrictions.

In recent years, as U.S. producers of hot-rolled steel, saccharin, polyvinyl alcohol, nonmalleable cast iron pipe fittings, and silicon metal were "winning antidumping relief" from import competition and being liberated to raise prices, their U.S. customers—producers of appliances, auto parts, foodstuffs, pharmaceuticals, buildings, and solar panel components— were bracing for disruptions to their supply chains and inevitable increases in their costs of production.

In the period from January 2000 through December 2009, the U.S. government initiated 304 antidumping cases. Of those 304 initiations, final antidumping measures were imposed in 164 cases. Intermediate goods—inputs consumed by U.S. producers in the process of adding value to make their own downstream products—accounted for 130, or 79.3 percent of the decade's antidumping orders. Yet, in none of those cases were firms in downstream consuming industries given a seat at the table. Under the statute, the authorities are required to ignore any potential impact of AD measures on downstream industries—and on the economy at large.

The 130 antidumping measures on intermediate goods can be broken out further to distinguish the 99 cases involving inputs used by manufacturers of goods and the 31 cases involving inputs used by non-goods-manufacturing producers, such as construction firms, utilities, and mining and drilling operations. Both sets of import-consuming producers suffer the costs and consequences of antidumping restrictions. Both pass some of those costs down the supply chain to the next level of consuming firms or end users in the form of higher energy costs, higher food prices, higher apartment and office lease rates, and higher input prices.

But the industries that rely on the inputs in the 99 manufacturing cases are those that are most likely to export. It is the companies in those industries which the president exhorts to "win the future." It is those firms who are competitively disadvantaged at home and abroad on account of the wayward U.S. antidumping regime.

What is most striking about these cases is the asymmetry between the size and economic importance of the petitioning industry and the adversely affected downstream industries. For 35 of the 99 AD orders imposed on manufacturing inputs, the entire petitioning industry consisted of just one firm. Yet the ensuing trade restrictions affected dozens or hundreds of downstream firms in numerous industries. For example, in 2005, on behalf of a single producer, the U.S. government imposed antidumping measures on imports of a widely used industrial ingredient called purified carboxymethylcellulose (CMC) from Finland, Mexico, the Netherlands, and Sweden. CMC is an input for production processes in 17 downstream industries (according to USITC [US International Trade Commission] descriptions). Those combined industries accounted for $172 billion of exports and 2.6 million employees in 2010. In stark contrast, U.S. exports of CMC in 2010 amounted to only $35 million. Yet the tail wags the dog.

In 2003, on behalf of a sole domestic producer, antidumping duties were imposed on imports of the artificial sweetener saccharin from China. Saccharin has widespread uses in the production of various food and beverage products, pharmaceuticals and medicines, as well as cleaning compounds. U.S. producers in these downstream industries accounted for $249 billion in U.S. exports in 2010 and employed 1.9 million workers. Meanwhile, U.S. exports of saccharin in 2010 came to slightly more than $7 million.

The fact that a single U.S. producer of a crucial manufacturing input can prevail in its efforts to limit its customers' access to alternative sources of supply should raise some eyebrows among policymakers. The fact that it is routinely the case that the antidumping law affords suppliers the ability to assert market power over their customers without any consideration of the economic consequences should be a wake-up call for those who fancy themselves stewards of sensible economic policy.

U.S. Foreign Trade Zones Encourage U.S. Production

Under the U.S. Foreign Trade Zones [FTZ] program, some of the costs inflicted on downstream, import-consuming firms can be mitigated. (Of course, the program wouldn't be necessary if U.S. duties were recognized as just another cost of production and set, optimally, at zero.) Among the aims of the FTZ program is to encourage manufacturing activity in the United States (and to discourage manufacturers from shuttering domestic operations and moving offshore as a result of the burden of paying U.S. customs duties).

FTZs are usually manufacturing plants or facilities physically located within the United States, but considered outside U.S. territory for the purpose of customs duty payment. Goods that enter FTZs are not subject to customs duties (including antidumping or countervailing duties) until they leave the zone and are formally entered into the commerce of the United States. If those goods are used as inputs to a further manufacturing process, the rate of duty applicable to the final product is assessed. If the goods are exported from a FTZ, with or without further processing, no duties are imposed because the product never officially "entered" the United States.

With respect to products made from materials and components subject to AD or CVD duties, the standing regulations require FTZ operators to get advance approval from the Foreign Trade Zones Board if the intention is to sell those final products in the United States. That requirement *does not apply* when the final product is going to be exported from the FTZ, which provides some incentive to downstream U.S. firms to keep production in the United States by operating as a FTZ.

Asking American firms to invest and hire, while simultaneously pushing policies to raise the cost of those activities, reflects either profound cynicism or incompetence.

But now the Obama administration—at the behest of the antidumping petitioners' bar and organized labor, and despite its own exhortations to U.S. companies to double exports, invest in America, and put Americans back to work—is proposing to seal off that channel of sanity and compromise. New regulations would require advance approval even if the final product was going to be exported.

The requirement of advance approval from the FTZ Board, which is administered within the Import Administration—the same agency at the Commerce Department that simultaneously assists protection-seekers in crafting their AD/CVD petitions, while gleefully implementing and administratively adjudicating the antidumping and countervailing duty laws—will tip the balance in favor of outsourcing production for many firms in many industries. Any benefits of continuing to produce in the United States will be diminished next to the rising costs and uncertainty of doing so.

Thus, companies like Dow Corning, which uses silicon metal to produce silicone components for solar panels, will have that much more incentive to shutter operations in Kentucky and set up shop in Canada or elsewhere, where silicon metal is available at lower prices, so that it can compete in foreign solar panel markets with Chinese, Japanese, Canadian, and European rivals.

Asking American firms to invest and hire, while simultaneously pushing policies to raise the cost of those activities, reflects either profound cynicism or incompetence.

U.S. Tariff Reform

At a time of growing concern over the competitiveness of U.S. firms, when even this administration claims to be looking for ways to streamline regulations and reduce other burdens on businesses so that they will invest and hire, it is hard to believe that reform of the U.S. tariff schedule, with its $20 billion burden on U.S. producers has been ignored. It is utterly absurd that antidumping reform has not only been overlooked, but that Commerce has proposed to strengthen the law as part of the NEI. Likewise, it makes no economic sense to subvert the purpose of the U.S. foreign trade zones program, which is intended to encourage domestic economic activity and to dissuade offshoring of production.

The fact is that antidumping measures, as well our normal MFN tariffs [lower tariffs imposed on imports from "most favored nations" (MFN)—typically World Trade Organization members], represent a huge drag on the competitiveness of downstream, value-added U.S. producers and a subsidy to foreign downstream, valued-added producers. None other than U.S. Trade Representative Ron Kirk made that point in the

U.S. WTO [World Trade Organization] case against Chinese raw material export restrictions earlier this year [2011]. He said:

> China maintains a number of measures that restrain exports of raw material inputs for which it is the top, or near top, world producer. These measures skew the playing field against the United States and other countries by creating substantial competitive benefits for downstream Chinese producers that use the inputs in the production and export of numerous processed steel, aluminum and chemical products and a wide range of further processed products.
>
> These raw material inputs are used to make many processed products in a number of primary manufacturing industries ... These products, in turn become essential components in even more numerous downstream products.

How can President Obama be serious about improving U.S. competitiveness when his Commerce Department is seeking to strengthen antidumping rules and the Foreign Trade Zones Board is moving to foreclose, or at least complicate, zone activities that use inputs subject to AD/CVD to make final products that are exported? How can we allow the president to throw nearly $100 billion in subsidies to solar, windmill, and lithium ion battery technology, while his policies make it more difficult to secure the necessary ingredients to produce and compete in those industries?

Let me conclude with an observation from the astute, mid-19th century French economics writer Frederic Bastiat. In 1850, he wrote:

> Between Paris and Brussels obstacles of many kinds exist. First of all, there is distance, which entails loss of time, and we must either submit to this ourselves, or pay another to submit to it. Then come rivers, marshes, accidents, bad roads, which are so many difficulties to be surmounted. We succeed in building bridges, in forming roads, and making

them smoother by pavements, iron rails, etc. But all this is costly, and the commodity must be made to bear the cost. Then there are robbers who infest the roads, and a body of police must be kept up, etc.

Now, among these obstacles there is one which we have ourselves set up, and at no little cost, too, between Brussels and Paris. There are men who lie in ambuscade along the frontier, armed to the teeth, and whose business it is to throw difficulties in the way of transporting merchandise from one country to the other. They are called Customhouse officers, and they act in precisely the same way as ruts and bad roads.

With no intended disrespect to CBP [Customs and Border Protection] officers or employees—it's only a personification of bad policy—this is what we have done. We have overcome the physical barriers—the bad roads, the swamps, the oceans, and shallow harbors—only to erect our own barriers. In a perfect world there would be no duties at all. The costs of imports, including duties, are production costs for firms and living expenses for families. Policies that portend to improve prospects for U.S.-based production and U.S. families should aim to reduce those costs, not increase them.

10

Spotted Again in America: Textile Jobs

Cameron McWhirter and Dinny McMahon

Cameron McWhirter covers regional politics and news from the Wall Street Journal's *Atlanta bureau. Dinny McMahon writes about China's banking and financial sector for the* Wall Street Journal *from Beijing.*

With costs rising overseas for textile manufactures, some companies are moving their operations to the southern United States. Manufacturers are finding that the savings on import duties and energy more than makes up for the higher cost of labor in the United States. The US southeast once held a bustling textile industry, and although there will not likely be a complete resurgence, many good jobs are returning.

Zhu Shanqing, who owns a yarn-spinning factory in Hangzhou in China's Zhejiang province, is struggling with rising costs for labor, energy and land. So he is boxing up some of his spindles and moving.

To South Carolina.

Mr. Zhu is one of a growing number of Asian textile manufacturers setting up production in the U.S. Southeast to save money as salaries, energy and other costs rise at home. His company, Keer Group Co., has agreed to invest $218 million to build a factory in unincorporated Lancaster County, not far from Charlotte, N.C.

The new plant will pay half as much as Mr. Zhu does for electricity in China and get local government support, he says. Keer expects to create at least 500 jobs.

There is another benefit. As costs continue to increase in China, Keer can ship yarn to manufacturers in Central America, which, unlike companies in China, can send finished clothes duty-free to the U.S.

The move by Mr. Zhu and others will scarcely revive a once bustling Southern textile industry. But it illustrates how shifts in global trade are creating advantages for U.S.-based manufacturing.

"We are on the leading edge of a mature cycle" with rising costs pushing Asian companies to consider moving to the U.S., said Robert Hitt III, South Carolina's commerce secretary.

In October, Mumbai-based ShriVallabh Pittie Group announced it would build a $70 million yarn operation in rural Sylvania, Ga., bringing 250 jobs. The company wants to avoid paying U.S. duties and to secure "cheap, plentiful and importantly reliable" energy, crucial in yarn production yet erratic in India, said Zulfiqar Ramzan, vice president for international development. Yarn spinning runs 24 hours a day, seven days a week, for most of the year, and any energy disruptions cause substantial delays and waste, he said.

In April, Alok Industries, another Mumbai textiles producer, said it would build a yarn-spinning factory in the South, though it hasn't said where.

Rising costs have made it more expensive to spin yarn in China than in the U.S.

The company expects to save on duties by making yarn in the U.S. and pay less than 10% of what it pays for energy in India, said Chief Executive Arun Agarwal.

In September, JN Fibers Inc. of China agreed to build a $45 million plant in South Carolina that turns plastic bottles into polyester fibers used to stuff pillows and furniture. That investment is expected to create 318 jobs. Development officials in South Carolina and Georgia say more Asian textile manufacturers have contacted them this year.

Rising costs have made it more expensive to spin yarn in China than in the U.S., said Brian Hamilton, a 2012 doctoral graduate of North Carolina State University's College of Textiles, who wrote his Ph.D. dissertation on the global textile industry.

He found that in 2003, a kilogram of yarn spun in the U.S. cost $2.86 to produce, while it cost $2.76 to produce a kilogram in China. By 2010, however, it cost $3.45 to produce a kilogram in the U.S. and the cost in China had jumped to $4.13 per kilogram. U.S. production costs were lower than Turkey, Korea and Brazil.

The new investments bring only a few jobs to a textile industry that all but died in the late 1990s, as many mills shut down or moved overseas for cheaper labor.

In November, 114,900 people worked in U.S. textile mills, a sharp decline from 1993, when 477,300 people worked in the mills, according to the U.S. Bureau of Labor Statistics.

U.S. duties on imported yarn and clothing have existed for decades. But trade pacts such as the North American Free Trade Agreement created duty-free zones between the U.S. and several trade partners.

In those agreements, the U.S. imposed a "yarn forward" requirement, meaning that textiles imported from partner countries have to be made completely from material produced in those countries or the U.S.

If not, they face duties, usually ranging from 5% to 6% for yarns, 10% and 12% for fabrics and 15% to 20% for clothing, according to the National Council of Textile Organizations, a U.S. textile trade group.

For years Asian clothing producers just swallowed the duties because production and transport costs were so low. Now they are reassessing that practice.

Mr. Zhu at Keer said that U.S. duties figured into his decision to set up shop in the U.S. so that he could take advantage of cloth makers in Central America, and not be solely dependent on an increasingly expensive China.

Mr. Zhu said that in Hangzhou—one of China's wealthiest cities—industrial land prices have soared, making expansion difficult. China's textile industry is plagued by overcapacity, which has squeezed margins, and local governments are reluctant to sell land to producers.

U.S. labor costs outstrip what Keer pays in China, but that difference will shrink as Chinese salaries keep rising, said Mr. Zhu, adding that he expects the gap will be more than compensated for by other savings.

The company settled on South Carolina's Lancaster County in part because of the proximity to Charlotte's banks and the port in Charleston, S.C., he said.

Lancaster County, which once had 11,000 residents working in textiles and now has 8.1% unemployment, has set an annual fixed fee in lieu of taxes that Keer will pay for 30 years.

Sixty percent of that annual fee will be returned to the company each year until it has paid off a $7.7 million bond that the county issued to help buy the land, said Keith Tunnell, president of the Lancaster County Economic Development Corporation. The state also provided benefits.

ShriVallabh Pittie Group plans to finance its plant with loans at interest rates much lower than it could get in India, plus generous state and local tax breaks and other benefits, Mr. Ramzan said.

The yarn spun at the new plant, about 50 miles north of a port in Savannah, Ga., will be shipped to Latin America to be made into clothing that can then be shipped back to the U.S. duty-free, he said.

"It's been a barrier to access," Mr. Ramzan said of U.S. duties. "As an Indian company, you have to try to make everything for 12% to 15% less to make a profit. Now we won't have to do that."

11

Made in the USA Is More Hype than Reality

Edward Hertzman

Edward Hertzman is the founder and publisher of Sourcing Journal.

There is a lot of discussion in the media about the return of apparel manufacturers from overseas to the United States. The reality, however, is that it is still much less expensive to make clothing overseas. Some consumers are willing to pay a premium for US-made clothing, but most are looking for current fashions at low prices. There simply isn't enough financial incentive for companies to return apparel manufacturing operations to the United States.

At every conference or trade show I attend, there is one question that's always asked: is apparel manufacturing returning to America?

In recent years, there has been a considerable amount of media attention focused on companies said to be "re-shoring" production back to the US. Walmart, the world's largest retailer (and one known for its vast global sourcing chain), made a major media splash when it pledged to sell more US-made goods in order to boost domestic manufacturers, while Everlane, a small venture-backed e-tailer known for its "radical transparency", has attracted attention for its practice of highlighting each of its factory partners on its website, many of them based in America.

While I find these examples interesting, a resurgence of manufacturing in America seems highly unlikely. Don't get me wrong; American apparel manufacturing does exist. In fact, I am wearing an American-made pair of twill pants from Adriano Goldschmied right now. And Adriano Goldschmied is not alone in manufacturing in the US. American Apparel, J Brand, Save Khaki, Karen Kane, New Balance and many others all have domestic supply chains in place. But to assess the real potential of a return to domestic production, we have to be honest about the facts.

In the past two decades, apparel imports to the US have surged 160 percent from $35 billion to $91 billion and now comprise an estimated 95 to 97 percent of all apparel sold at retail. In 2013, apparel imports grew 4 percent, measured by dollar value, over 2012, faster than the overall apparel market. What's more, companies have been consistently shifting production away from China, where labour costs continue to rise, to even cheaper countries like Vietnam and Bangladesh. In 2013, apparel imports from Vietnam, for example, grew by 14 percent (compared to 2.5 percent for China).

This doesn't mean niche premium brands cannot create healthy, profitable businesses producing domestically and selling to socially-conscious, patriotic or otherwise discerning consumers. But, realistically, only a small fraction of American consumers are willing to pay premium prices for US-made apparel. The majority of consumers think of fast fashion, discount retailers, dollar stores and coupons when it comes to purchasing clothing. Country of origin is simply not top of mind.

I have been in many meetings at apparel retailers where the topic of discussion has been lowering the cost of their goods. The solution, more often than not, is exploring alternative sourcing from countries in Asia. In the context of cutting cost, no company of any size has ever asked me how to bring production back to the US.

My stance on American apparel manufacturing is very simple: it won't work at scale because of simple economics. US cut-and-sew wages have increased by more than 13 percent in the past seven years (inflation adjusted) to an average of $14.79 an hour. Let's assume an average workday is eight hours. That comes to $118.32 per day, a figure that stands in considerable contrast to wage rates in low-cost countries like Bangladesh and Vietnam.

> *The reality is that no matter how much costs increase to accommodate better working conditions, labour costs in America will always be higher.*

In the past year, Bangladesh's government has finally agreed upon a new salary structure for its workers, which took effect 1 December 2013, bringing the nation's new [monthly] minimum wage to 5,300 taka ($68), a 77 percent increase from the previous minimum wage of 3,000 taka ($39), yet still the lowest worldwide wage rate in the apparel industry. Meanwhile, workers in Vietnam saw a monthly minimum wage increase to between VND 1.9 million and VND 2.7 million ($90 to $128) depending on the region, a raise of 15 to 17 percent over the previous year. In India, depending on the region, monthly wages range from $130 to $150.

This means that, despite the increases, in one day an American worker will earn what a Bangladeshi worker earns in two months, or an Indian worker earns in roughly one month. And while working conditions in low-wage nations have been under scrutiny since the terrible Rana Plaza building collapse in Bangladesh last year—and things are improving—the reality is that no matter how much costs increase to accommodate better working conditions, labour costs in America will always be higher.

Of course, US employers have to follow building codes and pay social security taxes, workers' compensation, health

insurance and overtime. What's more, underperforming workers often have to be documented by human resources departments and given multiple warnings before they can be replaced. And if a factory in America fails to follow the rules,
there are serious legal consequences, not to mention the likeli-
hood of negative national media coverage. By contrast, let's
just say, if a factory in Cambodia needs its workers to push
out extra units to make a delivery and save the factory from
forking out dollars to send their goods by air, the factory
owner won't need to do much to get these workers to stay and
work those extra hours. For apparel companies weighing their
sourcing options, all this makes doing business domestically
cost prohibitive and complex.

I am certainly not praising the often subpar labour conditions that exist in the Third World, but this is the reality. And
if retailers are currently responding to rising costs in China by
taking their business to Bangladesh, how is it even conceivable
that they will produce in the US?

But let's put aside wages for the moment. Since its incep-
tion, clothing manufacturing has always attracted unskilled
workers. From New York's garment district to Japan, Korea,
China, India and, now, Bangladesh, production has always mi-
grated from one low-cost country to the next based who could
offer the most competitive price.

Why would America want to "re-shore" an industry that is
having a hard time paying its workers $100 a month in the
Third World? Should we not be training and developing the
future American workforce for higher skilled manufacturing
where the better education and training many workers receive
in the US could offer us a competitive advantage?

Over the past decade, US textile and apparel employment
has plunged by nearly 50 percent to a record low of 363,000
jobs. According to the US Bureau of Labor Statistics, there are
only 110,000 cut-and-sew apparel workers in the country, a
number that has been consistently declining each month, so

apparel factories that have remained here in the US are facing a labour shortage, which is more than a bit ironic as one of the major reasons many give for supporting domestic apparel manufacturing is job creation.

This article may turn heads. I may seem pessimistic or unpatriotic, but I am trying to be honest and realistic about the prospect of bringing apparel manufacturing back to the US. I look at the world not through a domestic lens, but a global one. And if America is indeed to see a surge in domestic apparel manufacturing, it will be because its engineers and scientists develop new machinery and new software that can automate, speed up and lower the costs of production, thereby enabling the country to compete with the likes of low-cost Bangladesh. There is opportunity here. But are we allocating our energies and resources to the right battle?

Organizations to Contact

The editors have compiled the following list of organizations concerned with the issues debated in this book. The descriptions are derived from materials provided by the organizations. All have publications or information available for interested readers. The list was compiled on the date of publication of the present volume; names, addresses, phone and fax numbers, and e-mail and Internet addresses may change. Be aware that many organizations take several weeks or longer to respond to inquiries, so allow as much time as possible.

American Association of Exporters and Importers (AAEI)
1050 17th St. NW, Suite 810, Washington, DC   20036
(202) 857-8009 • fax: (202) 857-7843
website: www.aaei.org

The American Association of Exporters and Importers (AAEI) is a trade organization representing US companies engaged in global trade. AAEI advocates on behalf of US companies on trade policy issues before the US Congress and on trade compliance practices and operations before the World Trade Organization and the World Customs Organization. AAEI provides education to international trade compliance professionals through its committees that review proposed trade policy and regulations for comment, off-the-record webinars with government officials, and an annual conference, seminars and trade briefings. AAEI also provides information concerning government regulations through its international trade ALERT and annual Benchmarking Survey compiling the data on import, export, security, and product safety issues. Further information on these and other projects can be found on the group's website.

American Society for Precision Engineering (ASPE)
PO Box 10826, Raleigh, NC   27605-0826
(919) 839-8444 • fax: (919) 839-8039
website: www.aspe.net

The American Society for Precision Engineering (ASPE) promotes the future of manufacturing in America by advancing precision engineering through support for education and encouraging the development and application of precision principles. ASPE members represent a variety of technical areas—from engineering (mechanical, electrical, optical, and industrial) to materials science, physics, chemistry, mathematics, and computer science—and are employed by industry, academia, and national labs. ASPE, founded in 1986, is a nonprofit organization. The ASPE website includes links to recommended readings, the journal *Precision Engineering*, and its various newsletters.

American Society of Mechanical Engineers (ASME)

2 Park Ave., New York, NY   10016-5990
(800) 843-2763
e-mail: CustomerCare@asme.org
website: www.asme.org

The American Society of Mechanical Engineers (ASME) is a nonprofit membership organization that enables collaboration, knowledge sharing, career enrichment, and skills development across all engineering disciplines, toward a goal of helping the global engineering community develop solutions to benefit lives and livelihoods. ASME's membership includes more than 130,000 members in 158 countries—from college students and early-career engineers to project managers, corporate executives, researchers, and academic leaders. ASME serves this wide-ranging technical community through quality programs in continuing education, training and professional development, codes and standards, research, conferences and publications, government relations, and other forms of outreach. The ASME website includes press releases, latest news articles, and copies of its newsletters.

Association for Manufacturing Excellence (AME)

3701 Algonquin Rd., Suite 225
Rolling Meadows, IL   60008-3150

(224) 232-5980 • fax: (224) 232-5981
website: www.ame.org

The Association for Manufacturing Excellence (AME) is a nonprofit organization that offers its four thousand members a multitude of valuable resources to help them stay abreast of current industry developments, and improve the skills, competitiveness, and overall success of their organizations. Members range from executives to senior and middle managers who wish to improve both their organizations' and their personal performance through AME's forums, where members can stay current with new and developing management and operations techniques, and through *Target* and *Target Online*, the organization's publications. AME also holds annual international and regional conferences, monthly webinars, seminars, workshops, and tours. More information on all of AME's activities is available on the group's website.

Association for Manufacturing Technology (AMT)
7901 Westpark Dr., McLean, VA   22102-4206
(703) 893-2900 • fax: (703) 893-1151
e-mail: AMT@AMTonline.org
website: www.amtonline.org

The Association for Manufacturing Technology (AMT) represents and promotes US-based manufacturing technology and its members, which include those who design, build, sell, and service the continuously evolving technology that lies at the heart of manufacturing. AMT helps its members by providing access to markets in the United States and around the world and producing industry intelligence that aids businesses in making informed decisions. The AMT website is host to numerous informational resources, including public policy updates, presentations and webinars, reports on the manufacturing industry, and back issues of its monthly *AMT News*.

Buy American Project (BAP)
PO Box 780839, Orlando, FL   32878-0839
(888) 876-9633

e-mail: info@buyamericanproject.org
website: www.buyamericanproject.org

The Buy American Project (BAP) is a nonprofit organization that exists to create awareness of the benefits of supporting American-owned companies through education and advocacy. To that end, BAP works to create an encouraging economic atmosphere that strengthens American companies by working with and educating employees and officials of the United States. BAP is also actively pursuing a Buy American media campaign. Information on these efforts as well as on the newly formed Congressional Buy American Caucus is available on the organization's website.

Council on Competitiveness

900 17th St. NW, Suite 700, Washington, DC   20006
(202) 682-4292 • fax: (202) 682-5150
e-mail: communications@compete.org
website: www.compete.org

The Council on Competitiveness is a nonpartisan and nongovernmental organization of corporate executives, university presidents, and labor leaders working to ensure US prosperity. Together they act to increase US competitiveness, while generating innovative public policy solutions for a more prosperous America. Council members have access to partnership and networking opportunities through invitation-only policy dialogues, conferences, and events both in the United States and abroad. Information on the Council's initiatives, which includes the Innovate: Manufacturing program, is available on the organization's website. Additionally, the Council's publications are available for download in PDF format and are free of charge.

National Association of Manufacturers (NAM)

733 10th St. NW, Suite 700, Washington, DC   20001
(202) 637-3000 • fax: (202) 637-3182
e-mail: manufacturing@nam.org
website: www.nam.org

The National Association of Manufacturers (NAM) is the largest manufacturing association in the United States, representing small and large manufacturers in every industrial sector and in all fifty states. NAM is the voice of the manufacturing community and the leading advocate for a policy agenda that helps manufacturers compete in the global economy and create jobs across the United States. Publications available through the website include a blog, the digital magazine *Member Focus*, policy briefs, economic reports, and global manufacturing reports.

National Center for Manufacturing Sciences (NCMS)
3025 Boardwalk, Ann Arbor, MI   48108
(800) 222-6267
e-mail: info@ncms.org
website: www.ncms.org

The National Center for Manufacturing Sciences (NCMS) is a nonprofit, member-based consortium that exists to drive the global competitiveness of North American manufacturers through collaboration, innovation, and advanced technologies. As a neutral, impartial third party, NCMS is able to manage collaborative research projects, protect intellectual property, and ensure that funding is properly allocated and applied. The NCMS website includes information on the organization's projects, programs, and events, as well as press releases and a blog.

National Council for Advanced Manufacturing (NACFAM)
2025 M St. NW, Suite 800, Washington, DC   20036
(202) 367-1178
website: www.nacfam.org

The National Council for Advanced Manufacturing (NACFAM) is a nonpartisan think tank that brokers collaboration among its stakeholders from manufacturers (small, medium, and large), education, research entities, government, trade and professional associations, and individuals to develop policy recommendations to accelerate manufacturing innovation and build a more globally competitive US manufacturing sector. NACFAM also does projects to improve the bottom line and sustainability of manufacturing organizations. Information on current policy initiatives and projects, including sustainable manufacturing, are available on the organization's website.

Reshoring Initiative
e-mail: info@reshorenow.org
website: www.reshorenow.org

The Reshoring Initiative is an industry-led effort to bring manufacturing jobs back to the United States. The initiative works with US manufacturers to help them recognize their profit potential as well as the critical role they play in strengthening the economy by utilizing local sourcing and production. The Reshoring Initiative takes direct action by helping US manufacturers realize that local production and sourcing often reduce their total cost of ownership of purchased parts and tooling. The initiative also trains suppliers to demonstrate to these manufacturers the economic advantages of local sourcing. The Reshoring Initiative Library—a comprehensive list of articles, white papers, and case studies about reshoring, including examples of companies that have reshored—is available on its website.

Society of Manufacturing Engineers (SME)
1 SME Drive, Dearborn, MI   48128
(800) 733-4763
website: www.sme.org

The Society of Manufacturing Engineers (SME) serves practitioners, companies, educators, governments, and communities across the manufacturing spectrum. Through its strategic areas of events, media, membership, and training and development, SME shares the knowledge needed to advance manufacturing. Additionally, SME operates the SME Education Foundation, whose mission is to prepare youth for advanced manufacturing careers through outreach programs encouraging students to study science, technology, engineering, and mathematics, with a particular focus on technology and engineering. SME's website contains information on its numerous resources, including books, DVDs, an iTunes app, e-newsletters, research publications, technical papers, and more.

Bibliography

Books

Chris Anderson — *Makers: The New Industrial Revolution.* New York: Crown Business, 2014.

Joyce Oldham Appleby — *The Relentless Revolution: A History of Capitalism.* New York: W.W. Norton Co., 2010.

Suzanne Berger — *Making in America.* Cambridge, MA: MIT Press, 2013.

John Bowe — *Nobodies: Modern American Slave Labor and the Dark Side of the New Global Economy.* New York: Random House, 2007.

Bill Clinton — *Back to Work: Why We Need Smart Government for a Strong Economy.* New York: Random House, 2011.

Thomas L. Friedman and Michael Mandelbaum — *That Used to Be Us: How America Fell Behind in the World We Invented and How We Can Come Back.* New York: Farrar, Straus and Giroux, 2011.

Steven Greenhouse — *The Big Squeeze: Tough Times for the American Worker.* New York: Knopf, 2008.

Daniel T. Griswold — *Mad About Trade: Why Main Street America Should Embrace Globalization.* Washington, DC: Cato Institute, 2009.

Ron Hira   *Outsourcing America: What's Behind Our National Crisis and How We Can Reclaim American Jobs.* New York: American Management Association, 2005.

Tim Hutzel and Dave Lippert   *Bringing Jobs Back to the USA: Rebuilding America's Manufacturing Through Reshoring.* New York: Productivity Press, 2014.

Tim Hutzel and Paul Piechota   *Keeping Your Business in the U.S.A.: Profit Globally While Operating Locally.* Danvers, MA: CRC Press, 2011.

Joel Kurtzman   *Unleashing the Second American Century: Four Forces for Economic Dominance.* New York: PublicAffairs, 2014.

Hod Lipson and Melba Kurman   *Fabricated: The New World of 3D Printing.* Hoboken, NJ: Wiley, 2013.

Beth Macy   *Factory Man: How One Furniture Maker Battled Offshoring, Stayed Local—and Helped Save an American Town.* New York: Little, Brown and Company, 2014.

Peter Marsh   *The New Industrial Revolution: Consumers, Globalization and the End of Mass Production.* New Haven, CT: Yale University Press, 2013.

David E. Nye   *America's Assembly Line.* Cambridge, MA: MIT Press, 2013.

Mark Payne   *How to Kill a Unicorn: How the World's Hottest Innovation Factory Builds Bold Ideas That Make It to Market.* New York: Random House, 2014.

Martin Sieff   *That Should Still Be Us: How Thomas Friedman's Flat World Myths Are Keeping Us Flat on Our Backs.* Hoboken, NJ: Wiley, 2012.

Vaclav Smil   *Made in the USA: The Rise and Retreat of American Manufacturing.* Cambridge, MA: MIT Press, 2013.

Nick Taylor   *American-Made: The Enduring Legacy of the WPA.* New York: Bantam Books, 2008.

Periodicals and Internet Sources

Kyle Alspach   "The Robots Aren't Here for Our Jobs—At Least Not in Manufacturing," BetaBoston, August 18, 2014. http://betaboston.com.

Raveena Aulakh   "I Got Hired at a Bangladesh Sweatshop," *Toronto Star*, October 11, 2013.

Ben Baden   "Skills Gap Plagues US Manufacturing Industry," *U.S. News & World Report*, October 24, 2011.

Matt Brooks   "U.S. Olympic Uniforms Spark Fury in Congress," *Washington Post*, July 13, 2012.

Jian Deleon | "Ralph Lauren Makes 2014 Olympics Gear in America; Highlights Dire U.S. Manufacturing Situation," *GQ*, October, 29, 2013.

Eva Dou | "Robot Wars: Why China Is Outmanned in Electronics Automation," *Wall Street Journal*, August 24, 2014.

Rahm Emanuel | "Chicago's Plan to Match Education with Jobs," *Wall Street Journal*, December 19, 2011.

Rana Foroohar | "Detroit: America's Emerging Market," *Time*, August 28, 2014.

Thomas Friedman | "If You've Got the Skills, She's Got the Job," *New York Times*, November 17, 2012.

James R. Hagerty, John W. Miller, and Bob Tita | "U.S. Factories Keep Losing Ground to Global Rivals," *Wall Street Journal*, August 26, 2014.

Alexander E.M. Hess, Thomas C. Frohlich, and Alexander Kent | "10 States Where Manufacturing Still Matters," *24/7 Wall Street*, August 5, 2014. http://247wallst.com.

Emmarie Huetteman and Elizabeth A. Harris | "Walmart Fund to Support US Manufacturing," *New York Times*, January 23, 2014.

Daniel J. Ikenson | "Why NOT Make Olympic Uniforms in China?," CNN, July 15, 2012. www.cnn.com.

James Manyika and Katy George — "Opinion: Dispelling Myths About Manufacturing," *Washington Post*, April 30, 2013.

Michael Martinez — "Technology, Skills Moving Auto Industry Forward and Creating Jobs," *Detroit News*, August 4, 2014.

Salman Masood, Zia ur-Rehman, and Declan Walsh — "Hundreds Die in Factory Fires in Pakistan," *New York Times*, September 12, 2012.

Bill McKenzie — "Texas Faith: Should Americans Boycott Sweatshops in Places Like Bangladesh?," *Dallas Morning News*, May 23, 2013. http://religionblog.dallasnews.com.

Racheal Meiers — "The Other Women's Movement: Factory Workers in the Developing World," *HBR Blog Network*, May 28, 2013. http://blogs.hbr.org.

Martin Moylan — "Retailers, Including Target, Grapple with Unsafe Foreign Factories," Minnesota Public Radio, August 5, 2013. www.mprnews.org.

Floyd Norris — "Manufacturing Is Surprising Bright Spot in US Economy," *New York Times*, January 5, 2012.

Robert Portman — "Closing the Skills Gap," PortmanSenate.gov, May 10, 2013. www.portman.senate.gov.

Toh Han Shih "China Looks to the US for Low-End Manufacturing," *South China Morning Post*, August 11, 2014. www.scmp.com.

David Sirota "An Effort to Revive Manufacturing Through Redefinition," OregonLive, August 7, 2014. www.oregonlive.com.

Tanya Somanader "Chart of the Week: Auto Production at Its Highest Rate Since 2002," *White House Blog*, August 21, 2014. www.whitehouse.gov.

Jim Tankersley "Innovation: The Jackpot for American Manufacturers," *Washington Post*, April 30, 2013.

Chris Tomlinson "US Manufacturing Needs More than Cheap Energy," *Houston Chronicle*, August 26, 2014.

Index

Franklin Pierce University

00206647

DATE DUE